ABOUT THE AUTHOR

In 1967 a fairly serious illness put Jenny Wood in hospital for seven weeks and with this time on her hands she started to write the story of her family's life on the Island of Herm. Writing in longhand she continued the story up to 1972 when the first edition of 'Herm our Island Home' was published. She has now written of the following years to bring the story up to date. Educated at The Mount School, York, Mrs. Wood spent the war years as a F.A.N.Y. in S.O.E. She has been a member of the Ladies Ski Club since 1939 and in 1936 together with her brother was the first person to water ski in Britain.

Mrs. Wood was born in Yorkshire. She has six children, three sons and three daughters, and her present tally of grandchildren is twelve.

During the summer of 1991 Jenny Wood died suddenly, with all her family around her.

Sadly missed by her family and friends, 'Herm Our Island Home' and indeed the island itself, are lasting memorials to her life.

As 'Herm Our Island Home' goes to be reprinted in 1994 her words at the end of the book are as true as when she wrote them.

HERM
Our Island Home

Jenny Wood

for Peter with Love

First published in Great Britain by Robert Hale & Company, 1972
© Jenny Wood 1972
Reprinted May 1973

First NEL Paperback Edition February 1975
Reprinted May 1981

First Linton Ltd paperback edition March 1986

First published by Herm Gift Shop, Herm Island, Channel Islands, 1994

ISBN 0 9511187 0 6

Printed and bound in Great Britain by
The Guernsey Press Co. Ltd., Guernsey, Channel Islands

ACKNOWLEDGEMENTS

My thanks are due to Michael Marshall and to Victor Coysh for their help when I wrote the first edition of this book.

Throughout however I have been especially indebted to Dr. Stanley Kellett-Smith who, over many years, has made the fullest possible study of everything to do with Herm, its people, industries, every aspect of its history. His meticulously detailed notes in the Priaulx Library, Guernsey, have been of inestimable help.

My thanks also to Jo and Pennie who deciphered my handwriting and laboured long hours to produce the finished manuscript. To them also my thanks for their thumb nail sketches which occur throughout the book, and to Rupert for designing the cover.

Most of all my thanks to Peter, for his support and help and without whom there would have been no story to write.

SOME PRESS OPINIONS

On the 1972 edition.

"Mrs. Wood tells her real life adventure story with humour and honesty. Immensely readable, this is the book for anyone who has dreamed of a dream — and would like to dare to see it come true."

Time & Tide

"Herm: that enchanting speck of land off Guernsey so winningly described in Jenny Wood's *Herm, Our Island Home*. Mrs. Wood is to be envied for owning this delectable isle and applauded for writing so entertainingly."

Field

"Jenny Wood tells the story of an enchanting island, crossed by a single road, and crowned by tall pines."

Leeds Evening Post

"*Herm, Our Island Home* is a sort of diary — a sort of topographical exercise as well, and a guide book — a splendid combination for those who either know or don't know Herm. That Jenny Wood is a keen naturalist is quite apparent from the painstaking way she describes the plants, the birds and so on of Herm."

Bruce Parker, *BBC Radio 4*

"A fascinating modern adventure story."

Yorkshire Post

FOREWORD TO THE NEW EDITION
by Leslie Thomas

This is a lovely story, about a lovely island written by a lovely lady. Jenny Wood and her husband Peter have been running Herm for almost forty years — it would not be too much to say that this splendid couple *are* Herm.

When they first landed on this delightful little speck, just after Peter's return from the war, it was covered with a jungle. They had to hack their path through the overgrowth to reach the interior and discover the buildings that had all but been swallowed up during the years of the German occupation. All that Herm is today, its gentle ways, its comfortable habitations, its fine beaches have grown from the most unpromising beginnings. The miracle is that in bringing the island within reach of the people who now visit it, that they have succeeded in retaining its marvellous feeling of peace.

I collect islands like some people collect stamps. Nothing pleases me more than to see an island sitting in the sea and to be able to go ashore, explore it, and perhaps write about it afterwards. I first stepped onto the quay at Herm seventeen years ago when I was writing my first travel book — Some Lovely Islands. Since then I have been to many isles in widespread parts of the World — in the Pacific, the Atlantic, the Mediterranean, in Australia and in Japan. Herm remains one of my favourites and I am glad that Jenny Wood has decided to re-publish and update this warm and wonderful story.

THE LEGAL DISPOSITIONS OF HERM ISLAND

No record other than their stone tombs, remain to tell of the obviously well established social order which Neolithic man must have had on Herm over 4,000 years ago, but from the time of Christ the Island's legal dispositions down the centuries are fairly well documented.

———

PRE 6th C.A.D.	Within Roman Province of Constantia (now the Cotentin).
6th C.	Breton landlords, under the Frankish Kings.
933–940+	Passes to the Duke of Normandy and held by various Norman Seigneurs, Anschetel, Ranaulf I, II, and III and Mont St. Michel.
1204	Crown of England. King John.
1445–1737	Henry, Duke of Warwick, granted Lordship of the Isles, Herm being within the fief of Guernsey. From then on, Herm became a sporting reserve for the Governors of Guernsey to 1737.
1670	Adv. P. Gosselin, introduced sheep.
1717–1737	C. Nowall of London.
1737–1815	In turn, Peter Carey I, Peter Carey II, Caroline Carey, Peter John and Thomas de Jersey, John de Jersey, and Pierre Mauger.
1815–1826	The Hon. Col. J. Lindsay.
1830–1867	In turn, Jonathan Duncan, Ebenezer Fernie, Job Henry, Stephen Touzeau, Thomas Bartlett, and Thomas Hyde.
1867–1877	Col. M. J. Feilden.
1877–1881	In turn, James Considine, Arthur Maxwell.
1881	Trappist Monks (occupation not legally confirmed).
1882–1884	Chartreuse Monks.
1884–1889	James Linklater of Leith. Projected fish factory.
1889–1917	Gebhard Lebrecht, 3rd Prince Blücher von Wahlstatt.
1917–1920	Wheadon and Co. — farming.
1920–1923	Sir Compton Mackenzie.
1923–1939	Sir Percival Perry, later Lord Perry.
1940–1945	German Occupation.
1946–1949	A. G. Jefferies.
1949–	Peter and Jenny Wood.

1

We Find our Island

As soon as it was light we left the house and walked through the trees down the winding road to the harbour.

There wasn't much to say.

We passed through the silent shattered village and reached the harbour and then we turned and looked back. The road was littered with seaweed, splintered stone and beach pebbles, so that we had to watch where we put our feet.

The roofs of the cottages were all awry and most of the windows were black and empty, blown in by the force of the blast from the mine which the night before had floated almost into the harbour on the rising tide and detonated with devastating force just 40 yards from the end of the mole, and only 100 yards from the centre of the village. Stark against the skyline, 600 yards away, we could see that one of the barns was a skeleton, all the tiles blown off.

It was the 4th January 1952, and the British government had announced on the 30th December 1951 that the English

Channel could now be regarded as free of wartime mines. Just four days ago. Ironical.

"Peter, what does this mean to us?" I asked at last.

Peter was looking at a gap 4 inches wide which had appeared in the end of the harbour wall where the massive granite stones had been forced apart, and his voice was grim as he answered, "Last night when I was down here after this happened I went into the office and looked through our insurance policies. This kind of thing—war damage—is specifically excluded. It even mentions sea mines. We are not covered in any way."

He looked back at the little harbour village—so important to our lives now, and his face reflected our thoughts. We had been on the island two and half years now—our own island—and had put our all into it. Money, effort and, more important still, our dreams. Was this to be the end of it so soon after it had started?

To explain why we went to live on Herm, an island just 1½ miles long by ½ mile wide, I need to go back quite a long way. I think we had both been conditioned to the idea for years—indeed for me it began in my childhood which I spent in the little village of Linton-on-Wharfe in the West Riding of Yorkshire.

It was a pretty, peaceful place, a village in a valley, a village of grey stone houses and cottages, their roofs of strong, weathered slabs of Yorkshire stone, where golden lichen and emerald moss found a ready hold. We lived in the manor house, my parents, two brothers, my sister and I. In the garden there was a small lake on which my brother Geoffrey and I kept a dinghy and we spent endless hours playing there. We fished for minnows and frogspawn, dredging them up in a jamjar, and watched the water boatmen skidding busily around across the surface of the water. If I close my eyes and let fancy carry me back I can still smell that unique 'pond' smell. Other more realistic maritime adventures came on our annual summer holiday, frequently to Sark, where we spent long days exploring caves and rock pools, and swimming and diving in the astonishing sapphire depths of Venus Pool.

North-westwards from Sark lay another island, Herm. We used to gaze across to it and it seemed to us to be a magical place, sloping from the southern end gently down to a sweep of golden beaches to the north. We could see green fields and woods. Distance lent it a hazy enchantment—and it seemed to float above the placid sea. With my mind full of Tennyson's *Morte D'Arthur* I used to picture it as:

> The island valley of Avilion;
> Where falls not hail, or rain, or any snow,
> Nor ever wind blows loudly; but it lies
> Deep meadow'd, happy, fair with orchard-lawns
> And bowery hollows crown'd with summer sea.

One day we chugged across to the island in a fishing boat. We wanted to land and explore it but were told that it was private and belonged to a novelist—Compton Mackenzie. We were fascinated. To own an island! Surely this was the ultimate in possessions. I think that is when—for me—the seed was sown. I was half unaware of it, but from that moment on I think I must have cherished an ambition one day to live on an island of my own.

I had a very happy childhood—looking back I think of my early years as being endless summertime, a summertime which expanded until it was engulfed by the long winter of the war years, lightened for me when I became engaged to Peter. He was a New Zealander and had spent his childhood on a sheep farm in the North Island, before coming, in his early teens, to live in Wiltshire. His war service was chequered and exciting and almost entirely spent overseas, but it had somehow left him time in which to dream. I had joined the F.A.N.Y. as a wireless operator in S.O.E. and moved around from one closely guarded secret station to another.

We wrote regularly to each other, filling in those countless details about ourselves that we'd never had time to tell, writing what we were allowed to of the present and building dreams and plans for after the war. Always the same theme ran through Peter's letters. He had been trained to care for and take charge of his men, both in their duty hours and in their leisure time, and he felt that whatever he made of his life after the war he wanted to be deeply involved in the lives of those who worked for him; he felt that his responsibility should not end when the men left him at five o'clock and went home to their own particular problems and worries.

He had worked, prior to being called up, as a civil engineering contractor in Devonshire and one of his ideas at this time was that when he returned to his job after the war he would try and operate from a large country house estate in the South rather than from the centre of a city. Much of his work took him afield in any case, and he felt that not only would nothing be lost on an accessibility score, but that he might even be able to operate more efficiently. He would keep with him his key men, foreman and tradesmen, and one of their first tasks would be to construct houses for themselves on the estate.

This conception had something of the old lord of the manor or feudal system about it, where Peter, as a sort of father figure, would be not only responsible for the community's employment but would be concerned in his employees' well-being out of working hours, so that they were treated as individuals and important members of a community, not mere ciphers in a machine.

Peter is, however, a realist as well as a visionary and he saw this scheme as being not only satsifying to him as a man but capable of being run on very profitable lines.

He was demobilised in 1945 and we were married in Linton in the spring, on an April day of midsummer heat and sunshine. The garden at the manor where we wandered about with the wedding guests was ablaze with daffodils and spring flowers and the willows round the little lake were springing into tiny green leaf.

Our first home was an old converted farm-house in Linton,

4

only a quarter of a mile or so away from the manor house where I had lived. It stood surrounded by fields, gay with meadow flowers—I remember particularly the riot of golden buttercups.

Although the whole house—which was called College Farm—belonged to us, one half of it was occupied by tenants of the previous owner. As the law stood they were entitled to remain there unless alternative accommodation could be offered to them. We were not greatly concerned; there were only the two of us and the two-bedroomed cottage with which we were left was easily large enough for us; we decided to let matters rest as they were for the time being.

In the first year or two of our marriage, in the general scramble that ensued after the war to establish oneself firmly and securely in a job, Peter's wartime dreams and plans were shelved and he took up a job in my father's firm of motor engineers in Leeds. The firm was starting an agricultural department and Peter took over this, commuting there daily by car.

The work went well, but we always resented the daily parting, the necessity that drove Peter with each mile that he travelled farther away from his home. We had just spent five years away from each other, and quite apart from that we shared a common belief that one got married to be together, not to fly apart on different pursuits of one's own so that one's lives became two eccentric circles flinging away from each other with different interests, even different friends.

We bought a golden labrador dog so that I wouldn't be lonely in the long hours while he was away, and whenever Peter's work took him to outlying farms and villages, which it not infrequently did, Sapper, the dog, and I would accompany him. But being a camp-follower wasn't so easy after Simon was born, during the winter of 1946. For me this didn't matter too much, for interest and delight in the new baby kept me happy and occupied, but Peter continued to resent the many hours spent away from his home.

That was the winter of the great snow—it started in the New Year and was still with us in March. There was little sun, and day after day, week after week passed surrounded by negative colours of white, black and grey. And it was cold, bitter cold. When the late spring at long last came our minds turned more and more to the land, and when a chance came to buy back 35 acres which had once belonged to College Farm, it didn't take us very long to decide to buy it. And so, in addition to Peter's work, we started to farm, albeit in a pretty small way.

Whenever we could spare the time we were in the fields. Whether actually working or just walking about in it, we felt an enormous delight in knowing that this little bit of England really belonged to us. We hired a tractor and as the days lengthened Peter was able to put in several hours' work ploughing in the evenings, indeed he was often still at it long after nightfall, with the headlights of the tractor raking the night sky as he swung round to commence another furrow.

Peter's dreams began again. What if he could begin to operate an agricultural business from our farm? Could we gather about us a few key men and build houses for them on our own land? We schemed and planned and then discovered that the fields were scheduled as agricultural land and could not be built on.

And then a series of events occurred which certainly contributed towards shaping our future. Our second child, a daughter, Jo, was born. Delighted at achieving a pigeon pair we decided that the time had come to get possession of the other half of our house. We found a little cottage in the next village less than 2 miles away and bought it. We put about a few necessary repairs and redecorated it and then offered it to our tenants. It was a charming little place and, we felt, ideally suited to their needs. But the law thought otherwise. The local tribunal decided that the exigencies of the housing situation required that we continued to share College Farm, thus freeing our converted cottage to

6

house another family. We reluctantly saw their point, but from that moment we felt unsettled.

In the summer of 1949, in our growing restlessness, we sought some respite by visiting Peter's parents at Ox Barn, their lovely thatched home in Wiltshire. One morning as Peter walked in the nearby town of Warminster his father bade good morning to someone across the street.

"Who's that?" asked Peter idly.

"A man I know slightly," replied his father. "Name of Mr. Jefferies. He owns an island in the Channel Islands I believe."

Almost not knowing why, Peter remarked that he would like to meet him and asked his father if he could arrange it. Mr. Jefferies was invited for morning coffee the next day.

He arrived and brought with him an album full of photographs. He spoke about his island which he said was called Herm, and after coffee was over, opened the album to show his photographs. I drew in my breath sharply as he turned the pages.

"But I know that island!" I cried. "It's the one near Sark. I've sailed round it and it's *beautiful!*"

We pored over the pictures. Briefly he told us the history of the island. It had for years been a private estate, the hunting ground of the governors of nearby Guernsey, and later, in about 1890, the exclusive home of Prince Blucher von Wahlstadt. More recently it had been owned by Sir Compton Mackenzie, who later sub-leased the island to Lord Perry of the Ford Motor Company. Both Prince Blucher and Compton Mackenize had been Crown Tenants, as the island had belonged to the English Crown since Elizabethan days, as part of the Duchy of Normandy.

During the Second World War the island was virtually unoccupied, except for a caretaker and his wife, and from time to time a small garrison force of Germans. After the war Guernsey bought the island from the Crown and had let it on a long lease to Mr. Jefferies, the intention being that it was to be developed as a tourist amenity to Guernsey.

With a growing sense of excitement, which I somehow

knew Peter shared, I asked him if he lived there all the time and he admitted that he did not, business commitments in England kept him away from it for many weeks at a time.

"I tell you what," he said as he stood up, gathering his photographs together, "if you are on holiday with nothing special to do, why don't you go and see it for youself—there's a small hotel there, they'll put you up. And incidentally," he added, "if you like the place you can have it. It's on the market."

2

Moment of Decision

It was high June and a day of shimmering heat as we stepped ashore from the little fishing boat that took us across the 3 sea miles from Guernsey. A noon-day torpor hung over everything. An old horse stood between the shafts of a farm dray at the end of the tiny harbour and eyed us lazily. A youth in faded blue jeans lay on his back asleep in the dray and, apart from the ripples of water that the boat had made slapping against the harbour wall, nothing stirred. An oyster catcher suddenly whistled and piped somewhere along the shore and then was silent again.

There seemed to be no point in waking the youth with the horse and cart, so we picked up our suitcases and made our way along the quay to the little village and up a short path to a low, white colonial-style house which was clearly the hotel. We were expected and were shown to our room. We stood at the window and gazed out over the garden and lawn to the limpid blue sea beyond. It was incredibly beautiful. Little offshore islets were sprinkled along the coast which swept in a sickle curve of beaches to the north, but rose southwards to a high spur of land crowned with pine trees. Through the pines we glimpsed the round hump of the neighbour island of Jethou and the craggy outline of her little sister, Crevichon.

We watched our boat, a diminishing spot of white on the blue sea, returning to Guernsey, a hazy outline 3 miles away, then went downstairs to a cool white dining-room with gleaming oak tables, gay with marigolds, where we had lunch.

Later, armed with a small pictorial map that Mr. Jefferies

had given us, we set out to explore. We walked up the central drive which appeared to cross the island from west to east. The air was heavy with the hot sunny scent of gorse, but although the sun blazed down there was a refreshing movement of air slightly stirring the trees.

"I imagine one would never get a suffocating heat on a small island like this," remarked Peter, "there's bound to be some slight breeze off the sea."

We were climbing fairly steeply and rounded a corner beneath a clump of towering eucalyptus trees. I bent and picked up a crimson scimitar-shaped leaf and crushed it between my fingers and inhaled the pungemt eucalyptus smell. We found from our map that the field on our right was called Valley Panto. The names of the fields intrigued us—there was Moulinet, Bon Jour, Pan, Big Seagull, Little Seagull and Fairy Rings, Bramble and Monku. We wondered how they had come by their strange names.

We breasted the hill and passed between two high granite walls. The heat radiated from them, and the little hart's-tongue ferns and the green fleshy leaves of the pennywort springing from the crevices glistened in the sun. A cigale, an enormous grasshopper, flew on to Peter's shoulder, paused a moment and leapt away again. We came to a low parapet and leant on it and gazed down across the fields to the sea. The little harbour lay below us and a small green fishing boat fussed busily away from it towards Guernsey.

Down to our right and nestling under a bracken-covered hill was a diminutive cottage with a well-kept little garden surrounding it. A woman was watering her flowers and I was reminded of the cottage Tom peered down upon from the top of the cliff in "The Water Babies".

A path lay along the coast from the harbour, passed the cottage and wound out of sight around the hill. On the hill among the bracken grew tall cactus-like plants, their sword-like leaves spearing the skyline. There seemed to be the site of an old quarry and we remembered Mr. Jefferies telling us that granite had been extensively quarried on the island about a hundred years ago—he had told us that the Duke of

10

York steps in Waterloo Place in London were made of Herm granite. This was evidently one of the old workings but its rugged outline was softened now by trails of ivy and hanging moss.

A movement to our left made us look round. A grey donkey eyed us inquisitively round the corner of the wall. He was joined by another and together they advanced cautiously towards us. We leant over the wall and stroked their warm furry foreheads. Yet another arrived and soon, to our amazement, a herd of no less than ten donkeys jostled each other in front of us. We moved and they suddenly wheeled and cantered off down the field and out of sight beneath the bank. Mr. Jefferies hadn't mentioned them, and we wondered what were the implications of sharing the island with ten donkeys—we were to find out in good time.

Behind us lay a group of solid-looking grey granite buildings, obviuosly farm buildings, and we decided to leave these until later and to get a general impression of the island first. We continued along our path and presently came to a crossroads. To our right and left between stone walls ran a farm road which, according to our map, ran the length of the island from north to south. We crossed over it and descended a steep path through a field on the eastern side. Presently the field opened out into a verdant and lovely valley. Foxglove and willow-herb covered the slopes, and a backdrop of tall pines crowned the hilltops, with willows and blossoming elder bushes in profusion beside the way. A triangular gleam of sapphire-blue sea sparkled at the end of the valley. It was enchanting.

Soon the way divided and a small path, little more than a rabbit track, curved to the left and out of sight round the hill. We continued straight on and presently the path became steeper and ran down to the sea. Bracken-covered promontories thrust out into the sea enclosing a most perfect cove of firm golden sand which sloped gently to the water's edge. I don't think either of us had ever seen a more beautiful bay. It was sheltered, sunny and clean. 'Clean' was a word that constantly came to mind. Everything looked clean, shining clean; not only the sea sparkled with light but every leaf and blade of grass reflected glistening light and life.

We climbed back to the intersection of the path and turned north, breasting our way through chin-high bracken, and presently a curve of pale-yellow sand swept into view. It was so different from Belvoir, the cove we had just seen, that we stood and gazed in wonder. Here the cliffs had given way to open common land and the long beach we looked at might well have been a Bahamian strand, the colours of the sea and sand would have been no more vivid. The sand was much lighter in colour than at Belvoir and when we walked along it we realized that it was composed of myriads of tiny shells, some of exquisite colour and design. I bent down and picked up a tiny pink cowrie shell.

"We used to find these in Sark, I remember. I haven't seen one since."

Childhood memories swept over me and I turned and gazed back at the neighbour island lying to the east and thought how I'd once looked across to Herm and thought of it as Avilion.

We crossed the common and delighted in the tiny fragrant Burnet roses scrambling over the ground. Bright patches of thyme and lady's slipper were flung like a gay patchwork quilt across a slope to the west.

We climbed a sandy path and came to the central spine road running from north to south down the length of the island.

"It's almost impossible to realise the island is only one and a half miles long by half a mile wide," I remarked. "It seems much bigger."

We decided it was because of its great variety in so small a compass. Little valleys, woodland, farmland, common, sandy beaches and tall cliffs. The island really seemed to have everything. I drew Peter's attention to three black figures in the corner of a field.

"They look like nuns," I said to Peter. "I wonder where they have come from and if they are staying on the island."

12

As I spoke the three 'nuns' took flight and disappeared into a wood. Three crows! I found it astonishingly difficult to adjust to the small scale of everything; distances were most deceptive. Even now, after over twenty years, I am sometimes momentarily surprised how tall a person can look across a span of a field or two in this Lilliputian land.

At the south end of the island we came to the cliffs, a wonderland of nesting sea birds, clumps of pink sea thrift and white campion. Topaz-coloured lichen glowed on the grey granite outcrops of rocks. We watched a pair of puffins strutting importantly about a rocky spur, their bright orange beaks and astonished-looking eyes making us laugh.

We turned west and wandered back along a precipitous-looking cliff path and down a steep half-overgrown flight of steps cut in the cliff, and found we were looking down at a little landing place. Another steep flight of steps, this time cut in the solid granite, led through an ecclesiastical-looking archway to the sea. This was no doubt the landing used at low tide when the harbour was dry.

We wandered along a lane thickly bordered by honeysuckle and so presently came back again to the hotel. We sat on the lawn beneath a large shady umbrella and had tea.

"Isn't it beautiful," said Peter. "I have never known a place so peaceful." And it was true. Peace in Herm is a tangible thing; one can positively feel it.

I agreed. "I can see myself living a very pleasant lotus eating life here."

Peter laughed. "Well there wouldn't be much chance of that," he replied. "If you think that life here would be a rest cure that's the first illusion you'd have to get rid of. But," he went on, "it would be jolly interesting and a heavenly place to live in."

I glanced at him and realised that he was speaking seriously. One of us, I thought, is going to have to keep their feet on the ground; it was all too easy to fall under the spell of this idyllic island. Nevertheless, I felt a mounting excitement which was hard to subdue.

After tea we walked up the drive again, this time noticing

the camellia and rhododendron bushes, many of them sadly overgrown and struggling against the brambles.

"I'd like to get a scythe in among them to give them a chance," said Peter. Already we were beginning to feel possessive.

We made for the farm buildings and were pleased to find how solid and robust these appeared to be. Roofs were in sore need of repair in many places, but the walls were stout and looked as if, old as they were, they were yet good for many centuries to come. Hearing the chink of pails we turned into a cowshed where a girl was just finishing milking half a dozen Guernsey cows. Two little calves were in a pen to one side and I stroked their soft warm golden coats.

"They are quite my favourite kind of cow," I said.

Peter questioned the girl about the small herd and learnt that no other breed of cow was allowed in the island or in Guernsey. If ever a cow left the islands for any reason it was never allowed back again. For this reason the breed has remained essentially true and free from cross strains. I leant against the farmyard wall and was again struck by the warmth radiating from the stone, although it was now evening.

We turned out of the farmyard and were confronted by a solid, square, castellated keep. An arched passageway led round the side of it and following it round we became aware for the first time to some small degree of the task confronting whoever took on Herm.

A scene of enormous decrepitude and decay met us. The walls of the keep itself, built of huge granite blocks, appeared to be sound enough; but elsewhere there was a welter of buildings which were in a sorry state of repair—windows out, roofs fallen in, doors, if they remained at all, askew on their hinges, and the wood of windows and door frames rotten and decayed.

We came upon what had evidently been a blacksmith's forge. The anvil still stood there, the forge and an enormous pair of bellows, but otherwise only the walls remained. Wooden lean-to buildings leant drunkenly against each other, and everywhere was the accumulated rubbish of ages, including broken furniture, rusty kitchen utensils and crockery. And over everything the tangled growth of bramble and briar which spoke of years of neglect and decay.

We turned back, resolving to disregard the whole area in our assessment of the island's assets. As we passed the farmyard again the girl called to us to ask if we had seen the chapel and pointed to an arched doorway opposite. We pushed open the door with some difficulty, went in and found a perfectly proportioned little chapel of great charm and simplicity. But here again, neglect was evident. Damp discoloured the roof, dead leaves littered the floor and over the altar lay a stained and tattered altarcloth. Honeysuckle, ivy and briars struggled to push in through the windows, some of which were broken, and the door at the west end was jammed and ill-fitting. Nevertheless, it was a lovely little chapel. Outside the west door across a tangle of bramble and overgrown fuchsia bushes stood a belfry, detached from the church and housing, askew in its rusty mounting, a large bell.

I looked at Peter and quite suddenly knew what he was thinking. If ever there was a chance to make all those plans and dreams he had made during the war come true, then this island represented that chance. Here in this little chapel we would hold a family service on Sundays; we would have to have a school for the island's children, our own as well as those of people who would come to live and work for us on the island. There would have to be a central island office, for there would be public services, like a water supply, to administer, electricity to instal and roads to maintain. A host of thoughts raced through our minds, but they only seemed to harden our enthusiasm. As we made our way down the hill, we both realised that we were going to make every effort to get possession of this island.

After dinner that evening we sat on the lawn drinking our coffee, and talked about all we had seen. One thing was abundantly clear—that, although there was no denying the incredible beauty and natural charms of Herm, by taking it on we would harness ourselves to years of hard work and uncertainty. We were later to learn that in the few years before the war the level of maintenance had not been high. Some of the cottages had not been lived in since the early twenties, and during the war there had been no maintenance at all. Mr. Jefferies in his short tenancy had really only been able to renovate the main hotel building so that during the ten years from 1939 nothing had been done. Decay is progressive and once it gets going sets in apace. This clearly would be more so on a little island where every building is so exposed to sea air and storm.

Quite apart from the demolition or restoration of old buildings and their subsequent maintenance, if we were to support an existence on the island we would have to run it as a business and develop its almost non-existent tourist amenities. The hotel was excellent, but small, and would almost certainly have to be increased in size to make it a worthwhile venture.

I can remember now, and always will, the feelings I had at this time, when clearly a moment of big decision was looming up. I should have been thinking of the problems involved in bringing up a young family, cut off by 3 miles of sea from the nearest shops and medical care, without a telephone or even, as I was soon to find out, a proper water supply; but somehow, the only feeling I had was one of excitement at the thought of living on our own little island and that, incredibly enough, my childhood Avilion.

Later Peter told me that he'd never know why he didn't coldly assess the obvious difficulties of the task, the building up from the bottom of a varying number of businesses about most of which he knew nothing at all; but the emotion dominant in his mind at the time was the tremendous challenge it all represented, and he felt only a surge of determination to take it up, along with the immense attraction of having an island to call our own. Looking back, at the moment, it seemed to me that both our lives had been leading up to this moment of decision, so that it seemed easier to take up the challenge than to turn it down. If we were to let

16

this opportunity slip we would feel to be traitors to all our early schemes and dreams.

Next morning we were suddenly obsessed with a sense of urgency. How many other people might already be interested in the island? That afternoon we returned to Guernsey and flew back to England. We lost no time in driving down to Wiltshire where we sought out Mr. Jefferies. We discovered that we were indeed justified in thinking that there was no time to lose. Several other people had made inquiries and one at least was extremely interested. Immediately we put an option on the island; then, for the first time we sat back and seriously contemplated the step we were thinking of taking.

"You know," said Peter, "I think it would be a good idea if we were to consult your father about this."

It was a sound suggestion. We had always valued Dad's help and counsel. He was a shrewd and able businessman and would without doubt be able to assess the potential of the island from a business angle more ably than we. But Dad was in mid-Atlantic on his way home from America. We cabled his ship, saying merely that we had a matter of some importance to discuss with him, and a short while later back came his reply: "Meet you at the Royal Automobile Club, Pall Mall, Wednesday 11.00 a.m."

We were there half an hour before the appointed time and when Dad finally walked through the doors we rose excitedly to our feet. But Dad was calm.

"No, I don't want to hear anything yet. Not a word yet please!"

He strode into the drawing-room and summoned a waiter. He ordered coffee and settled us down in comfortable chairs, then proceeded to talk about his trip. We curbed our impatience. The coffee came and we drank it and still Dad continued to make small talk. At last he replaced his empty cup on the table and sank back in his chair and crossed his legs. With his eyes shut, hands in an attitude of prayer, fingertips resting on the bridge of his nose, a trick he had when concentrating deeply he asked, "Right, now what's on your minds?"

17

We told him. When at length we had finished he uncrossed his legs, stood up and glanced at his watch.

"How do we get there? when's the next plane?" he asked.

Within three hours we were airbourne and on our way back to Herm. This time we flew right over the island on our run in to Guernsey. The long sweeping curves of the northern beaches shone white in the sun, the sea creamed lazily around the cliffs to the south, and the green fields and paths stood out clearly and well defined. From the air Herm looked a verdant lovely place. Dad was impressed.

We spent two days on the island and showed him all we knew of it. When we came to the decrepit area behind the farm Dad was undeterred by the squalor and neglected and insisted on pushing his way through the undergrowth and rubbish and climbing the steep steps giving access to the keep itself. We pushed open the door and found a flight of steep rickety wooden steps. Each side of the steps was lined with empty gin bottles. Dad, a staunch teetotaller, regarded them distastefully, but proceeded up the stairs.

Opening a door at the top we entered a room. Again empty gin bottles littered the floor. Then we noticed an elderly gentleman seated by the window and were momentarily nonplussed. He rose to his feet, and noticed that his clothes were well cut, if slightly shabby, and his grey hair was neatly brushed. It was an incongruous situation. We apologised for our intrusion and explained that we had thought the place uninhabited. He told us that he had come to the island to help Mr Jefferies for the summer. We asked him what he did and he told us that he sold ice cream to the few visitors that came across daily from Guernsey. He was, he said, more or less camping in the keep, which had neither light, water nor heat.

The room in which we stood was tall and well proportioned. The windows to the south were arched and a fair size, but those to the north were mere slits cut in the thickness of the walls, and reminded me of the arrow slits in the city walls of York. The ceiling was heavily beamed with a golden-brown timber. He told us that Prince Blucher

18

had lived in the keep and adjoining manor house, which was now in such a bad state of repair that it was uninhabitable. Much of the timber used in both the keep and the manor house was Silesian pine, brought from the pine forests of the Prince's vast estates in Silesia. He had apparently done considerable building on the island during his time in Herm, and, though both the keep and manor were of a much older period, he had added a wing to the latter and also was responsible for the crenellations on the roofs of both.

We left the keep and ventured into the manor. It was, as we had just heard, in a truly appalling state of repair. Whatever it had been like in the Prince's day was hard to determine as some subsequent owner had carved the once handsome building up into a warren of ill divided rooms and corridors. It was a shambles of rotting partitions and falling plaster. The whole place even on this bright June day had a dismal damp air and we returned thankfully into the warm sunshine.

We made our way past the farm and the chapel to the lane. We leant our elbows on the low parapet overlooking the harbour where we had seen the donkeys on our first visit. The all important question was put at last.

"Well Dad, what do you think of it all?"

If we had hoped for a shrewd assessment of the business potential of Herm we were to be disappointed. Dad was silent for a moment and then he said, "There's really only one thing to be said—one question to ask. Could you be happy living here? Peter, could you be happy? Jenny, could you be happy?"

We tried not to answer impulsively and thought about it solemnly. And then, "Yes we could," we both assured him.

"Well then," he replied, "Have a go!" His blue eyes twinkled. "I know this," he added, "if I felt as you do and I was thirty years younger I'd have a go myself!" Our hearts leapt—it was all the encouragement we needed. We flew back to England and made arrangements to complete the purchase of the lease from Mr. Jefferies. Then north to Yorkshire to see our bank manager. With an effort we played down the

19

dramatic effect, matching our tone to his, as he asked how he could help us.

"We have bought an island," said Peter, "and we would like to offer it as security for an overdraft."

"An island?"

"One of the Channel Islands," I said, as though we had had the choice of several.

"Quite so," said the manager, his tone implying that it was all in a day's work; but I thought I saw the quickening of his interest.

Then, trying not to talk both together, we told him about Herm. Perhaps he also had a soft spot for islands, or pictured the bank in possession of their security; certainly he was sympathetic and helpful, and very soon, albeit with some trepidation—it was a thing we had never done before—we arranged a loan from the bank. I found myself thinking of Shakespeare's advice, "Neither a borrower nor a lender be," as we signed the various documents and I felt that I should never feel easy until we had paid back every penny.

However, these dealings with Mr. Jefferies and our bank were only preliminaries, as we were soon to discover, for the States of Guernsey would not agree to the sale until they were satisfied as to the ability of the people who were going to buy it to handle the job properly. Herm had been purchased by the States of Guernsey from the Crown in 1946, as an amenity to their tourist industry, so that the unspoiled charm and natural beauty of the island, which was considered to be unsurpassed in the Channel Islands, should be available to all who visited it. It had been recommended that the island should be leased to and be administered by enthusiasts ready to welcome visitors and to allow them reasonable freedom throughout the island and that the governing principle should be to ensure the preservation of the natural attractions and peacefulness of the island. The States had to assure themselves that Peter and I measured up as tenants.

Remembering that first solemn meeting in the Administration Chambers of the Government of Guernsey, I well recall noticing one of the members of the board gazing speculatively first at Peter then at me, and I was more than a little startled to hear him mutter to himself, "You poor people, my heart bleeds for you." I told Peter about it afterwards, but he thought I had misheard and, anyway, such was our enthusiasm that we dismissed the remark forthwith. Not only the States, but also H.M. Government were concerned in the new purchasers, and we had to be approved by His Excellency the Lieutenant Governor of Guernsey, at that time, General Sir Philip Neame, V.C. Hearing the frequent reference to the States I can recall saying to myself, "What ever have the States got to do with it?" But it wasn't long before I realised that the Government of Guernsey is called the 'States' and Uncle Sam had nothing to do with the matter at all . . . Guernsey is a Crown Dependency, and as such is self-governing, the Parliament being called the States of Deliberation.

Firstly we had to produce references, and these the States took up in great detail, so there was another pause. We passed this hurdle and subsequently were approved by His Excellency.

The next stumbling block was the terms of the lease. It was a full-repairing lease, and it was already obvious to us that we would never be able to keep our heads above water if, in addition to trying to make the island as a whole a viable business, we were to assume responsibility for all the running repairs, both external and internal. Added to these heavy financial obligations was a rent to be paid of £1,000 a year.

We decided that we must try and negotiate a fresh lease, rather than have the balance of the present lease assigned to us.

At our next meeting with the Board of Administration, the committee appointed by the States to deal with the affairs of Herm, it was suggested that the present lease should be scrapped. But how to draw up another lease, before there was any real information on which to base it? It seemed to be stalemate. We were unwilling to sign our names to the old lease—they to sign theirs to one based, as it would inevitably be, on so many unknown factors. We hit on a compromise.

21

We were to run the island without a lease at all for a trial period of a few years, and we were to maintain a set of accounts which would be scrutinised annually by the board, and, on the evidence they showed, a new lease would be drawn up to cover a period of time, no less than sixty-six years, with a possibiltiy of ninety-nine years, and with more realistic regard to the heavy cost of running the island.

Our own legal adviser, and Dad as well, were somewhat apprehensive about this arrangement—take on such a commitment and involve so much money without the security of a lease behind us? What if the political climate in the States of Guernsey should change and they should wish to dispossess us of the island? The arrangement appeared to violate every code of prudent business agreement. We recognised the risk element, but had complete confidence and faith in the board, who indeed approached our problems with a wise and fatherly attitude. We agreed to the arrangement and so at last the way was clear. We completed with Mr. Jefferies, confirmed our arrangements with the bank and Herm was ours.

3

First Problems

Once back in College Farm the business of packing up confronted us, and the next weeks passed in a whirl of activity.

One evening as we sat surrounded by packing cases and talking as usual about the move ahead, Peter asked for the twentieth time: "You're *sure* you're not going to be lonely?"

I reassured him, though admitting that in some respects I wished there was someone we knew going with us, chiefly because it was a formidable task to face on our own and we could do with some help. And then Peter had an idea.

"Philip! I just wonder whether there's any chance that Phil and Nina would consider joining us?"

Philip, Peter's brother, had recently married down-to-earth practical Nina, and had trained, like Peter, as a civil engineer. Since the war he had set himself up in a garage and repair business in the south and I thought it unlikely that he'd want to make the break just as his business was beginning to get established. Was it even fair to ask him?

"There's no harm in asking him," said Peter, getting to his feet.

"Yes, he can always say no. But it would be a grand thing if he came."

We were both enthusiastic and Peter went to the telephone, and there followed a long conversation, at the end of which Philip promised to ring us back the following night. We were sitting by the 'phone when it rang the next evening.

"Well?" said Peter. I heard Philip's voice as he answered.

"Nina says when do you expect to be there?"

Peter told him.

"We'll be there before you!" replied Philip, a man of few words and lightning decisions. We hung up the receiver and sighed with relief. We were excessively pleased. The thought of another pair of heads, two more pairs of shoulders to put to the task was immensely comforting and reassuring.

A week or two later came the moment of departure. The furniture had left and our car stood outside the door. I picked up Jo in her carry-cot and placed her on the back seat where she beamed expectantly. She was eight months old now, a contented happy child, game for any diversion from the normal. Sapper, the labrador, climbed in and sat protectively beside her. I settled myself in the front with Simon, now 2, who was all agog at the thought of the journey ahead, sitting on my knee. I waited for Peter and he eventually came.

"I've been waiting for you," he said reproachfully. "Surely you want to go round the house with me for the last time?"

I hadn't wanted to—I had wanted to make the break swiftly and cleanly, not think about it at all. I had always been good at the ostrich technique of burying my head in the sand whenever unpleasant moments came my way, but I dutifully got out of the car and followed him into the house and we made the nostalgic pilgrimage from room to room. I was filled with sudden dejection and depression. I

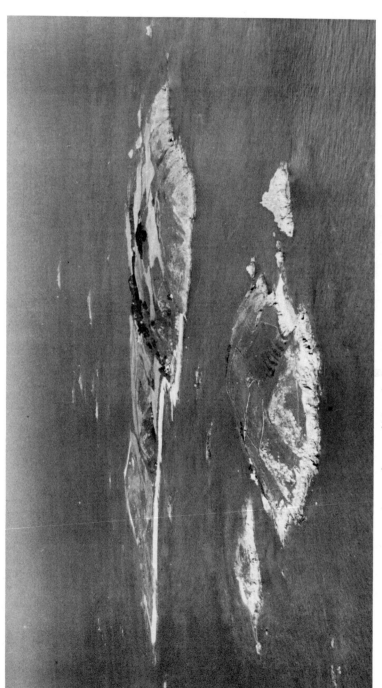

An aerial view of Herm looking N.E. over the Island of Jethou.

Simon's first view of the island.

Simon and Sapper on the foredeck of our first boat the 40-ton Vosper cargo launch built early '30s.

Simon, Jo and Sapper — 1950.

Peter, Simon, the cowman Bill and our very first calf.

Le Manoir — the Manor House and Keep, old Mill Tower, our house and gardens, the Manor farm buildings and cottages.

took my seat in the car again and we drove away in silence, sunk in our own thoughts and heedless of Simon's excited chatter.

"This is no good," said Peter after a while, "come along, brighten up, this is the start of all those plans we had—remember? This is going to be exciting and fun—hard work, yes, but rewarding too, I'm certain of it."

We pulled ourselves together and started to talk again. Next day we caught the mail steamer from Weymouth. Happily, it was a still, calm crossing, and as the coast of England slipped away behind us we settled down to enjoy the voyage. I remember how we put Jo in her carry-cot in a corner of the boat-deck guarded by Sapper and walked with Simon round and round the deck, all of us too excited to sit still for long. Sapper and his charge provoked a certain amount of interest and amusement among our fellow passengers, and more than one camera was levelled at the picture of canine devotion and attention to duty which he provided.

As we drew near the islands the colour of the sea deepened, and away on the horizon little drifts of white clouds appeared showing where the islands lay. We landed about five o'clock and made our way to the quay where we found the boat for Herm. She was called *Celia* and she lay alongside, piled high with our furniture and all our worldly belongings. And an incongruous cargo it looked too, with Simon's rocking horse perched rakishly on top—he was overjoyed to be reunited with it. We were somewhat dismayed to notice how lifeless and dull our furniture all looked, piled up in an undignified heap in the stern of the boat. We tried to reassure ourselves that, once assembled in a home again, its own comfortable and homely looks would be restored to it.

Twenty-five minutes later we stepped ashore in Herm. True to their word Philip and Nina were there to greet us and both had put in quite a lot of spadework to smooth our arrival.

The hotel was full of guests and the cottages were either in occupation by temporary staff who had come to work on the island for the summer or were in too sorry a state to be occupied at all. Philip and Nina were hard at work patching up one such cottage which stood on the cliffside above Rosiere, the low-water landing place, for their own use and had found temporary quarters for us in the Mermaid cottages, which lay by the sea about 100 yards along the coast from the hotel.

We planned to move into Fisherman's Cottage, the delightful little cottage under the hill, when it became vacant at the end of the summer, though we were a little perplexed as to how we would house all our furniture—it was considerably smaller than College Farm. In the meantime we must make do with two small rooms in the Mermaid. No good to try and fit any of our furniture into them—they were already furnished as bedrooms, so that all that remained to do was to put up the children's cots and have the rest of our belongings loaded on to a tractor and taken up to be stored in one of the large barns at the top of the hill.

Leaving me to settle in, Peter went off with Philip to look round. The rooms were dark; thick undergrowth and trees grew closely outside the windows and, with all our suitcases in the room, we seemed to be impossibly short of space. I sank down on the bed and for a moment was swept with despair. I thought longingly of our cosy farmhouse in Yorkshire, the cheery kitchen, the old beamed drawing-room and gay sunny morning-room opening out into the garden. And I had thought we were cramped at Linton! Jo smiled unconcernedly from her cot and Simon chased happily around. They at least were unperturbed.

Fortunately the children left me little time to repine or worry and I pulled myself together and set about seeing to their needs and sorting out things from the suitcases that we would require. At least there was the hotel where we should be able to take our meals, so really there were no problems that couldn't be got over once we had shaken down into our tiny quarters. The wardrobe was small and inadequate, so I slung a rope which had bound one of the cases across the room and hung many of our clothes on that, and another rope I slung across the opposite corner so

I could air Jo's nappies after washing them in the little bathroom across the corridor.

The washbasin, I discovered, produced only a trickle of water, but sufficient, if I was patient, to manage. By the time I had finished we looked like a group of mid-European refugees camping out in an attic—and this is the way it was for the first two months after our arrival.

Next day Peter warned me to be as economical as possible with the use of water; there was a serious shortage as a result of a long, hot, dry summer.

"There's nothing we can do about it yet," he told me. "But it will mean another well in the autumn."

Short of water and two children to look after! "Ah well, there's always the sea," I thought, and set off purposefully for the nearest beach, carrying Jo and followed by Simon. As the cold water closed round Jo's sun-warmed little body screams of indignant protestation rose from the sea, but I pressed grimly on until she was fresh and clean. Simon was more co-operative and obviously thought the new routine more fun than the normal wash and scrub.

Those first weeks on Herm were rather like a protracted summer holiday as far as I was concerned. Since we fed in the hotel I had no meals to prepare and therefore little to do beyond looking after the children, and I couldn't rid myself of the feeling that soon we would be packing up and returning home. For this reason I longed for the day when we could move into a house of our own. Then I knew, with our own furniture about me and in the establishment of a regular domestic routine, I should no longer feel adrift and would begin to put roots down and to feel that the island was really my home.

Hot sunny days followed each other without any sign of a break in the weather. The water situation was serious, but by exercising the strictest economy everywhere we just managed, although from shortly after our arrival, all through the rest of that long, hot summer we had to ship in water from Guernsey, herself suffering from a water shortage.

I saw little of Peter. He was abroad from first light,

27

seeing to whatever task seemed to claim priority at the time. There were boats to be unloaded, stores to order, a host of activities to organise and run—the inevitable run of minor crises such as a blocked drain or wastepipe, or a sudden water shortage at some key point, due to someone carelessly leaving a tap running.

The land began to have a dry, brown, parched appearance, and looked very different from the green, verdant island we had seen when we first arrived. One day Philip had an alarming experience. Noticing that a rubbish tip we had been using in the corner of 'Fairy Rings' was becoming unsightly he lit a match to set fire to it. Immediately the whole field virtually exploded and a flicker of flame shot across it. There must have been a film of highly combustible dry particles hovering over the field, which was triggered off by the lighting of a single match. Fortunately the fire was contained within the granite walls of the field and was short lived and didn't spread; but the incident alerted us to keeping a close watch on picnic parties. We bought a number of broad shovels with which to beat the flames in the event of another like episode. Happily it occurred again but once and that was when, years later, a misguided visitor purposely set fire to a gorse bush as an object lesson to his children and to illustrate just how easily gorse bushes burnt! The ensuing fire swept down the side of Monku hill, but mercifully burnt itself out in the long grasses bordering the beach and did no great damage, although the clouds of smoke sweeping the west coast of the island alarmed not only us, but many people in Guernsey, and the watch tower made enquiries immediately. The object lesson no doubt rebounded on the discomfited Dad!

Such staff as there were were a motley crew, disorganised and disinterested, but there seemed to be little point in making changes at this stage. All one could do was take notes and gain experience for the following season. The hotel was running smoothly enough and we were able to leave this to its own devices to carry on.

The small businesses started by Mr. Jefferies to serve the

visiting population from Guernsey were of a fairly rudimentary nature. Foremost among these was the Mermaid Tavern, a long low building adjacent to the cottages where we were living and reputedly once the haunt of smugglers. It appeared to do quite a lively business, especially with the local boatmen and fishermen.

Ice cream was sold by the elderly gentleman we had met in the keep. He operated from an open window at one end of the tavern, and cups of tea were dispensed from another window at the other end of the inn.

And then there were the donkeys! It seemed that the sole function of the youth we had seen asleep in the cart on our first visit to the island was to take visiting children for donkey rides in a long meadow beyond the Mermaid Tavern. Since the meadow was inadequately walled or fenced, he spent a considerable part of his time rounding them up each morning. They strayed far and wide, and more than a few of Peter's and Philip's 'minor crises' were involved in sorting out their misdemeanours. We were sceptical as to whether we would find it practical to continue with them next year.

Peter and Philip spent long hours that first summer tracing out the source of the water supply. They found it consisted of a number of wells in use, and another two, the use of which had been discontinued. These wells supplied only the buildings in their immediate vicinity, so that if one well failed, or was giving short supply, it was impossible to take advantage of one of the other wells other than by the laborious business of carting water from one place to another. It was obvious that in the autumn priority of activities must be given to establishing a more efficient water supply, operating, if possible, on a ring main connecting up all the wells; it sounded as if it would be a lengthy and costly business, but that it must be done was quite clear.

4

Lady Perry's Cottage

One evening after dinner, about a couple of weeks after our arrival, we were approached by a very engaging Irishman who introduced himself to Peter with the words:

"You know, you and I really ought to know each other."

"And why is that?" asked Peter.

"Because I'm a tenant of yours," replied the other. We were amazed. We had thought we were familiar with all of the few people resident on the island and knew of no other house or cottage where he might be living. He said he lived in Lady Perry's Cottage. We'd never heard of it, much less seen it. He invited us up there and then. We followed him up the hill and then, to our surprise, he turned along the arched passageway beside the keep and proceeded to pick his way through the rubbish and undergrowth beyond. We followed him down a single track, breasting our way through high grass and a tangle of bramble and briar until we came to a faded blue door in a high granite wall. We passed through it and found ourselves in a vast walled garden.

Apart from a diminutive area of lawn the whole garden seemed to be a wilderness of towering evergreen oak, overgrown euonymus and hydrangea bushes. They pressed in closely round a small cottage in front of which ran a wooden verandah shaded by a striped sun awning. No wonder we had never seen the cottage before, it was completely hidden from all aspects.

Our host led us inside and we looked round in amazement. Here was no tiny cottage parlour which, from the exterior, we would have expected, but a large, spacious, beautifully proportioned drawing-room. The polished wood floor was covered in gay rugs, a table in the centre of the room held a pot of bright geraniums and a copper jug of marigolds gleamed on the hearth of a pleasant low fireplace.

His wife, an attractive auburn-haired Irishwoman, rose to meet us and settled us into comfortable chairs. In the state of 'flux' in which we had been living, it was reassuring to see such an established home on the island and it filled me with a new sense of security. Coffee was served and as the Irishman handed Peter his cup he remarked, "I know exactly what you are thinking! You're thinking that this house would suit you and your family fine!"

Peter confessed that those were indeed his thoughts.

The Irishman laughed and told us that he was in fact leaving and returning to Ireland within a couple of months, so we were spared the unpleasant task of giving him notice to vacate while yet accepting his hospitality. We were both immensely cheered by this turn of events and the knowledge that within a matter of weeks we could look forward to moving into this delightful house. We were shown over it and found that although it presented a single-storey cottage appearance from the front it was in fact quite a sizeable house. The ground fell steeply away at the back so that at the other side it was three-storeyed.

There were two bedrooms upstairs, facing west and east respectively, and on the ground floor, besides the drawing-room there was a large kitchen. A flight of steps led downstairs to a larder and large cellar with bare earth floor.

The next day we returned again to explore the garden. I had always longed to live in a house with a walled garden and I was thrilled to know that at last I was going to do so. The garden covered about three acres and was badly in need of attention and some ruthless clearing, yet its very unkemptness was exciting. There were long tunnels crossing the garden from side to side where evergreen oak trees had met overhead in a dense tangle of branches, shutting out the sky, and one shuffled through a bed of accumulated fallen leaves.

In one corner was an overgrown rose garden, the bushes tall now and straggling up into the sky but many of them still bearing lovely blooms. Others had reverted to wild roses and most were being throttled by bindweed and ivy.

Another part of the garden had been laid out as an orchard. The trees were old and gnarled but had fruit forming on them. We came across a group of medlar and quince trees, another strange, exotic-looking tree with scarlet flowers whose name we didn't know, and several slender eucalyptus trees, this time with silvery, honesty-shaped leaves.

There was a large greenhouse in a bad state of repair and a long potting shed built against the garden wall. Further along this same wall was a line of fig trees, their branches untrained now and falling forward, their many-fingered leaves forming a backcloth of glossy green. The whole garden was a sheltered, quiet place with a wonderful atmosphere of peace and restfulness.

Along one side of the garden ran a long avenue of enormous pines, which led up to the central spine road of the island. Midway along another side and facing out to sea, on a little knoll, was a small round tower. It had, according to an old map we had seen, once been a windmill, but here again, we could detect Prince Blucher's handiwork. The original top had been replaced by a crenellated battlement, like the one on the keep and the front of the manor house. It was an attractive feature and overlooked the garden—it would make a fine summer house or playhouse for the children. In fact, many years later, it became a stable for their pony.

We have since discovered that this tower is marked on Admiralty charts as "The old Mill of Herm" and indeed is the only identifying mark shown on the island.

Both Peter and I were anxious that before the summer was over we should invite our relations over, so that they could satisfy their minds about the island where we had chosen to live and the sort of life we would be leading. We were well aware that, apart from Dad, most of our friends visualised Herm as a stark hump standing up in the sea, upon which we were faced with scratching a living. I think most of them thought we needed our heads read to even contemplate such an existence. We wanted them to come and see for themselves. We decided that after the last hotel guest left and before the staff were disbanded for the winter we would invite them over for a house-party, during the first week of October.

One morning, towards the end of September, we awoke to the hollow boom of the foghorn. A thick white mist had rolled in from the sea and we couldn't see the end of the garden. There was a remarkable stillness everywhere.

For ten days the fog never lifted and we were shrouded in a dense white enveloping pall. The sense of isolation and solitude was profound. The foghorn at the harbour mouth in Guernsey moaned continually, answered at intervals by the deeper, profounder note of the Platte Fougere, north towards Alderney. Occasionally the mist would coil back as far as Jethou, and we would see the island floating ethereally, strangely tall and spectre-like in the mist. From time to time our boat would creep cautiously into the harbour bringing much-needed supplies and as cautiously out again, guided back to Guernsey by the sound of the foghorn.

We began to be concerned about our house-party and wondered whether our guests would be able to get through to us. And then, on the last day of the month, we awoke to a sparkling September morning. The damp mist had settled the dust of the long, hot summer and everything looked clean, washed and shining. The grass glistened with a myriad dewdrops and the sea was a limpid translucent blue. The bracken was turning golden on the hills and never had the island looked more lovely. Flowers were in bloom everywhere: the drive up the hill was hedged on either side with pink Guernsey lilies—it was the first time we had ever seen these lovely shell-pink flowers on their deep ruby-coloured stems; dahlias glowed in the hotel flowerbeds, and tall blue agapanthus lilies marched down the lawn. Late honeysuckle flowered in the hedges and shining blackberries hung in thick clusters.

A couple of days later our guests all duly arrived and, just as we hoped, were entranced with the loveliness of the island.

On 3rd October we christened Jo in the little chapel of Saint Tugual. We picked armfuls of pink lilies to decorate the chapel, and trails of pale-blue plumbago which we found growing over the old walls in the walled garden. They looked lovely against the grey granite of the chapel. It so happened that one of the clergymen who had assisted at our wedding in Yorkshire was now a minister in Guernsey and he came across and performed the ceremony.

For the whole of the weekend the weather was warm and sunny and we picnicked and swam at Belvoir, and in the evening it was so warm that we could sit out on the lawn in front of the hotel, watching the lights come on in Guernsey to be reflected in long streamers of light across the water.

When the time came for our guests to leave, and we waved them goodbye from the harbour, I think they had all made a re-assessment of our chances of making a success of, and of being happy, living in Herm. I remember how, as the boat drew away and headed towards Guernsey, Peter and I turned back along the quay and how we felt that now—this moment—was really the start of our endeavour. Alone with the island, and with the summer season behind us, we could really get down to the hundred and one tasks that needed to be done.

And that's very much how it was. The first thing, of course, was to house ourselves adequately. Philip and Nina, with a certain amount of labour to assist, had succeeded in making the cottage at Rosiere habitable and it was now indeed a charming little place, perched as it was on the cliff above the landing place.

The Irish couple had now left Lady Perry's cottage and work had commenced on some necessary repairs to the roof. We decided to move in as most of the work to be done was of an exterior nature.

Our furniture was brought out of the barn and stacked on the little lawn outside the house, ready to be carried in. And then our luck turned and the weather broke. We bundled the furniture into the house any old way, to be sorted out later, and the long overdue rain streamed down from a leaden sky, saturating everything, seeping in under the tarpaulins on the roof, running down the walls and soaking into the floorboards.

The builders cried off and returned to Guernsey, saying they would return when the weather improved, and we went to work with buckets and mops and tried to kep the rain at bay. It rained for three weeks alomost without ceasing but, damp and difficult as it was, it did little to depress my soaring spirits at being at long last in our own home.

At last the weather improved sufficiently for the men to return and for the work to go ahead again. But work that first winter was never easy—always we seemed to be battling against the elements. If it wasn't rain it was wind. We were reaping the harvest of the hot, dry, windless summer and the law of averages was establishing itself. But at last the work on our house at any rate was completed, roofs were sound again and walls were damp-proof.

One of the more bizarre problems we had to contend with that first winter was the donkeys. No field was stock-proof enough to contain them and they roamed at will. Hardly a day went by but they were up to some scrape or another. They behaved just like a troupe of naughty children. They were inquisitive and loved company, and wherever work was going on there they would be, kicking over buckets, trampling in cement or trotting over newly laid concrete. They were up to every conceivable mischief.

I returned home from a walk with the children one day to find them in possession of the house. Simon was delighted. I was appalled. It must have taken over half an hour to get them out again, by which time the havoc was indescribable—after all, ten donkeys in one's house! At one stage one donkey was half-way up the stairs and I had to climb over the banisters above him and, grasping his head firmly, push him down again while he proceeded to be as clumsy and awkward about the business as possible.

After that, we regretfully decided that they'd really have to go and we made arrangments to sell them. We kept two for Simon and Jo and called them Humpty and Dumpty; we put them in a small field that we had made secure, and they were no longer a problem.

By the same token, Champion, the horse, was somewhat of a liability also. During the season he had desultory work, transporting visitors' luggage to and fro between hotel and harbour, but now he had little work to do and was also inclined to wander at large.

I remember one day Simon coming to me and remarking, "Champion's hungry so he's going to eat Jo."

Hurrying into the garden I found the huge horse with its head in Jo's pram, gently nuzzling her. Jo was round and cuddly, and no doubt presented the appearance of a toothsome morsel. He was one of the largest horses I ever remember seeing and it was thought he had been left behind by the Germans at the end of the war. Certainly he seemed to understand German words of command better than English ones!

One evening Peter was coming up the hill late at night. It was pitch dark and he hadn't his torch. He was suddenly aware of heavy breathing in front of him. He advanced slowly and cautiously and suddenly came up hard against a warm hairy surface. He had walked straight into Champion, but confessed that it had been a most alarming experience and that for the first time he knew what was meant by the hairs of the back of his neck standing up in fear.

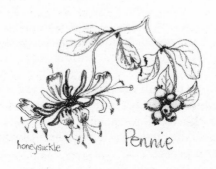

honeysuckle   Pennie

5

The Simple Life

The only electricity on Herm was supplied by an ancient D.C. generator housed in an old boat store down by the harbour. It served only the hotel and buildings in that vicinity and was a temperamental and unreliable source of supply at its best. It was not at all an unusual occurrence to see the lights in the hotel suddenly dim, brighten again, dim, brighten then extinguish altogether, whereupon there would be a mad scurry for candles and lamps. Fortunately the hotel guests would enter into the spirit of the thing and, far from complaining, would claim that the episodes lent atmosphere to their island holiday. But from Peter's point of view it was worrying and time-consuming whilst the fault was traced and repaired.

In our own house and all of the outlying cottages, including the farm, the lighting was by oil lamps. Looking back I am inclined to remember only the more attractive aspects of this; the warm and golden pools of light they cast, the long shadows, the friendly gleam of shining brass, and I forget the enormous amount of work they entailed. The inevitable times when I would come in with the children on a darkening winter's afternoon and remember that I had forgotten to replenish them with oil before setting out, the frustrating delay groping in the dark while I did so, and then—the lamp glasses! Labour-saving detergents were not yet on the market to any great extent and trimming the wicks and keeping the glasses bright and shining represented at least an hour's toil a day.

Oil lamps can be malevolent things. One could leave the room, carefully turning down the wick and return ten minutes later to find the room thick with black sooty fumes, the wick flaring wildly and the lamp glass inky black. They sorely tried the temper.

One evening Peter returned home tired and cold. As was our custom sometimes, he poured us both a drink and sat down with me by the fireside to talk over the day's happenings. It was a leisurely, comfortable time which we both looked forward to, with the children tucked up in bed and the house quiet and restful. Suddenly I was astonished to see him leap to his feet, clap his hand to his mouth and rush for the door into the garden. It was a minute before realisation struck. Only that morning, searching for a spare container for the paraffin I had carefully decanted it into an empty bottle and had carelessly left it on the sideboard. Peter swears he can recapture the taste to this day, and it was a long time before he could pour out our evening drink without a preliminary sniff at the bottle.

Ironing I did with flat-irons, heated up over the solid fuel cooking stove. I never found this a great hardship. I had two irons and one was heating up as the other was being used, and at least stood little chance of scorching things with an iron that was cooling down all the time one worked.

For the whole of that first winter we had no communication with Guernsey other than our boat, the *Celia*, which plied daily to the island unless the sea was too rough.

Our predecessor, Mr. Jefferies, in an effort to establish some sort of communication between Herm and Guernsey, had run a pigeon post service. Messages were written on a flimsy and attached to the bird's leg, and the pigeons then flew to a loft in Guernsey where the message was removed, and the bird was later returned by boat to Herm. The service was discontinued shortly after we came to Herm as, although it had for a year been, up to a point, effective, obviously some more efficient method of communication would have to be established.

All the same we were sometimes cut off for four or five days at a time so that I had to learn to keep a well-stocked store cupboard and to see that I always had plenty of flour. Not that I ever acquired any great skill at bread making—although I tried once or twice—but scones made a useful enough substitute in the absence of bread. Milk was no problem as we were plentifully supplied from the farm—with eggs also—and we grew our own vegetables.

Our boat, the *Celia,* was of neccesity moored over in Guernsey, since our own small harbour dries out twice a day, and to keep her afloat we would have had to move her to the Rosiere anchorage, sometimes impracticable because of weather conditions, and in any case a time-consuming operation. For this reason I longed for a telephone linking us with Guernsey, chiefly on medical grounds. I felt apprehensive at the slightest sign of any illness in the children and constantly dreaded the thought of an accident. Soon after our arrival we had such an accident when Simon slipped off a stool and cut his head sufficiently badly for it to require stitching. Most fortunately it occurred on a Sunday when a friend from Guernsey had come across in his boat to tea with us and he was able to take Peter back with Simon to the doctor.

We had an Aldis lamp and had been told that in the event of an emergency we were to flash it in the direction of the watch house at the harbour mouth at Saint Peter Port, but nothing had been arranged about passing messages with it and the assumption was that if we flashed it a boat would be sent out to find out what was the matter. It seemed to me as if there would inevitably be a long delay before medical assistance could arrive.

Philip had rigged up an internal system of communication with some old German army field telephone sets which he had found. A rather ungainly set of poles carried the wires from one point to another across the island, and his house at Rosiere and ours were in communication. This was some measure of reassurance to us that at least we could establish speedy contact with each other in the event of emergency. It had its social uses too.

On Sunday afternoon Nina rang through and asked us if we would walk over to tea with them. We arranged for someone from one of the nearby farm cottages to come in and look after the two children and we set off.

It was a wild blustery afternoon and it was cosy in Rosiere Cottage sitting by the fire. At about five o'clock as we rose to go a sudden flurry of rain rattled the windows and Nina urged us to wait until it had blown over. I readily agreed and asked Peter to ring through to the house to say that we were staying on for a little while. He went to the phone but when he twirled the handle could hear no ringing at the other end.

"That's funny, it was working perfectly when you rang through, Nina," he remarked.

I tried to reassure him by saying that no doubt the wind had brought down the wire, but Peter was uneasy.

"We'll go back now," he insisted. So off we went into the rain and near gale-force wind across the island.

We were drenched by the time we arrived back home. The children were both safe and sound, sitting by the drawing-room fire having a story read to them. The girl in charge of them confirmed that the telephone bell had not rung.

Peter, still uneasy, went off on a tour of inspection. A short while later, looking very agitated he ran into the room with the fire bucket and threw a load of sand on the fire, then dampened it with a bucket of water. When

40

he had extinguished it he ran for an axe and went down into the cellar below. The firebricks at the back of the drawingroom fire had become so intensely hot that they had ignited the timber beams of the floor which constituted the roof of the cellar.

The cellar was by no means draught proof and in that high wind it was just a question of time before the whole floor would have been ablaze. Peter was able to cut away the burning sections of the beams and they fell harmlessly on the earth floor beneath.

We felt it had been a narrow escape and the strange thing was that non-ringing of the telephone had had nothing to do with the fire. It was, in fact, the wind had brought the wires down, so it was just by chance that we had returned when we did.

This incident alerted us to consider our fire precautions, and everyone was briefed in their duties in the event of such an emergency. One night Peter called a fire drill practice—he hoped unexpectedly—but somehow news of it must have leaked out because when he ran out of the hotel door, banging a stick on a dustbin lid and shouting almost all the islanders emerged from one of the nearby cottages where they had foregathered to drink coffee and await the expected summons!

We rigged up a small hand-drawn cart as a fire-engine, with poles fore and aft, and the men practised running around the island with it to various places where fire might be expected to occur. Once it ran away going down the steep hill to Belvoir and as four men struggled to control it, Philip pounding along at his position on one of the front handles, glared at Peter who was running easily alongside. "You might help!" he gasped, but Peter refused. Later he explained, "I wanted to see if four people could manage it, or if it needed six. Obviously it needs six!"

Nowadays, as a fire alarm we ring the chapel bell continuously. One evening recently I heard it pealing and ran across the garden to the belfry. Grasping the startled bell ringer by the coat-tails I demanded where was the fire.

41

"Madam," he replied with dignity, "there is no fire that I am aware of—I am ringing the Angelus." A visiting cleric had sought and obtained Peter's permission to hold an evening service in the chapel, a rare enough occurrence to explain my mistake.

One rough winter evening we were awaiting the arrival of the *Celia*. Peter was aboard her and we couldn't understand what delayed her. Before daylight faded Philip had seen her through his binoculars leaving Saint Peter Port and she should have been in. The wind strengthened and darkness came down. We were greatly concerned.

"We'd better try the Aldis lamp," said Philip. "But there's not much point just flashing it, they'd have no idea what we want. Jenny, you know Morse don't you? You'd better come along and see if you can make them understand."

He fetched the Aldis lamp and together he and I climbed on to the roof of the hotel which faced directly towards the watch house at Saint Peter Port harbour. Standing there, buffeted by the wind and unable to hear ourselves speak I laboriously flashed out a message in Morse to the watch house. I informed them that the *Celia* was overdue, was she all right? Completely unused to either sending or receiving light signals, Morse to me, as I had practised it during the war, was an audible signal not a visual one, it was a long time before I could make head or tail of the dots and dashes flashed back to me. They must have repeated their answer a dozen times before, at last, I was able to report to Philip, "They say that *Celia* is safe and has returned to port." We were vastly relieved.

Next day we received an instruction from the harbour master to say that whoever had been operating the lamp in Herm *must* learn his Morse code properly. I was indignant. I knew my Morse code perfectly well, but was prepared to admit that I didn't know my Aldis lamp! I set about improving my knowledge of it and practising with it, but the occasion to use it never rose again, and within a few months we had the telephone.

It was, and still is, a radio telephone and, I believe, one

of, if not the smallest, fully automatic public telephone exchanges in the world. After our isolation it was a wonderful and incredible thought that now we could pick up the phone and, having dialled Guernsey, ask to be put through to any corner of the world. To inaugurate the line we put through a call to my sister who was in Sweden at the time and we heard each other perfectly.

It is now a much-used link with the outside world, and internally also it is extremely useful, as each trading department now has its telephone as well as several of the island houses. We also have an emergency link which operates on an independent electrical supply and which is used in the event of major power breakdown. We had to invoke this upon occasion, and only once has it let us down by breaking down itself, and then we were lucky as it was during the summer months and a radio-equipped visiting boat happened to be in the harbour at the time and radioed for the medical assistance we were seeking.

6

Paul

During that first autumn and winter and well into the following spring and early summer work went ahead to establish a more satisfactory water supply. We were most anxious not to go through another summer with a water situation such as had existed the previous summer, when we had been shipping in fresh water from Guernsey.

Whenever it was possible for them to do so labourers came across from Guernsey and Peter and Philip toiled with them to dig trenches and lay pipes so as to connect up the wells. Thus all the water could be brought to one place for purification and distribution. This measure, without the addition of an extra well, proved to be sufficient for the next two or three years, which was a relief as even this had been a costly enough undertaking.

As the winter days began to lengthen into spring we turned our minds to the coming summer season. It had been such a busy autumn and winter that we had few reserves of either cash or energy to make any changes in the hotel and it would have to carry on as before. We at least felt that we would have no great problems as far as water was concerned.

As far as amenities for the daily visitor went, all we could manage that first year was to consolidate all our catering efforts into one room at the far end of the Mermaid Tavern. We installed a tea urn and gas ring and sold cups of tea, sandwiches and cakes and ice cream. We engaged one or two university students during their long vacation to help us with the purely seasonal work, but regrettably these were not an unqualified success—they were far too inclined to regard the whole thing as either a rest cure on a holiday island, or a perfect opportunity to study long and furiously for their impending examinations. The experience strengthened our determination to build up a community on the island itself and to be as independent as possible of outside seasonal labour.

About this time a Frenchman, Paul, came to work for us. He was a countryman born and bred, and came to us from his native land of Brittany. He had worked through the summer season in the hotel as a kitchen porter, and then asked if he could remain on with us as a gardener, which he said was his real *métier*. He was an energetic and hardworking man and just the fellow we needed to attack the enormous amount of work that there was to do in the gardens.

There was, however, the problem of where he was to live. Comprising one wall of the farmyard was a row of eight cottages, but these were in an appalling state of repair and quite unfit for habitation. We decided to convert the row into four large cottages which would measure up to present-day requirements and it seemed that now was the time to start.

Before Paul could start on the gardens he would have to assist in putting one of the cottages to rights. We engaged a mason and labourers from Guernsey to help, and Paul and they went to work.

In the matter of a month or two one of the cottages was converted and Paul moved in with his newly acquired French wife. Work went steadily ahead on the other cottages, and exteriorly, at any rate, they were soon weatherproof and sound, though it is true to say that any new exployees we took on spent the first few weeks of their employment at work on the interior decoration of their cottage before they started work on the task for which they had actually been employed.

The system worked well and one quickly got the measure of a man's worth when faced with these initial labours of, so to speak, building his own house. Also, rightly or wrongly, we felt it gave new arrivals a feeling that they were carving a niche for themselves in the very structure of the island—a feeling of belonging to and identification wuth the island life.

We were fortunate at this time to come across some old photographs of the island, taken during Lord Perry's tenancy. They had been taken from the air and showed clearly how the gardens had been laid out. They must have looked superb. We had heard that he had employed ten gardeners and, although we didn't aspire to restore them to their former glory, we were able from these photographs to uncover many paths and rockeries we had no idea existed.

Paul was indeed a prodigious worker and the wilderness and thickets fell before his swinging axe and sickle. He worked so fast, however, that it was necessary to keep a close watch on his activities and, more than once, I saved a clump of graceful laburnums or a healthy lilac by flying from the house shrieking, *"Arretez! Arretez!"* just in the nick of time. I was too late, however, to save an aged mulberry tree which sprawled across the grass in lovely and fantastic shape outside our kitchen window. Simon and Jo were sad about this as they used to pretend it was a pirate ship and climb amongst its branches. I felt sad too, it had been *so* old and had stood there so long—but Peter assured me that it was just as well we'd been saved the awful decision to fell it because it was growing too near the house and besides obscuring a lot of light and view, was possibly bringing damp into the house.

Once the vegitation was cleared back we had a splendid out-look. Southwards we looked right across the walled garden and through the pine avenue to the fields beyond, where we could see the cows grazing. Westwards we looked out over the garden to the sea and Guernsey beyond. Our view spanned the whole sweep of the east coast from St Martin's Point in the south to L'Ancresse in the north.

The sea itself became an unending source of interest and delight. Never the same from one hour to the next, it varied in mood from gale to calm, in colour from deep violet through peacock shades of blue and green to palest aqua-marine.

Away to the north we could watch large ships on their way to America, and down to the south-west, in a triangle framed by the branches of a pine tree, we could see the gulls wheeling round the little conical-shaped islet of Crev-ichon. At night it was especially lovely to look across the water to the twinkling amber lights of Saint Peter Port, to watch the harbour lights change from red to white, and perhaps the green and red riding lights of ships lying at anchor off the coast.

oyster catcher

Pennie

7

First Island Baby

During our second winter on the island Penelope was born, the first child, so the records in Guernsey later told us, to be born in Herm for well over a hundred years. The telephone, great boon though it was, in those first years was inclined to be very temperamental because of the varying voltage of our electricity. If, for any reason, the voltage was low, it was impossible to establish contact with Guernsey. This was a little worrying as the expected time for the baby's arrival drew near. No good asking *me* to operate the Aldis lamp under the circumstances! So it was arranged that when the time came to call the doctor, if we were unable to get through on the telephone, Peter would light a bonfire on a prominent hill, clearly visible to the watch house and this would be a sign that we wanted the doctor.

Imagine our dismay then when the baby chose to arrive during the late evening of 5th November! Guernsey itself was ablaze with bonfires and fireworks and there is no doubt

48

that had we lit ours in Herm it would have been regarded as just another Guy Fawkes celebration!

Mercifully the telephone worked perfectly and the doctor came across within an hour. Not, however, without a certain amount of difficulty because, in addition to it being rough and blowy, as ill luck would have it, that night was one of the biggest spring tides of the year. It was low tide when the boat arrived at the Rosiere landing and there was insufficient water for it to come alongside. Bearing his bag above his head and carrying his shoes and stockings, the long-suffering doctor had to roll up his trousers and wade ashore. Nor were his difficulties over then. The baby perforce had to be delivered by the light of oil lamps, and anyone who has experienced working close to one of these will appreciate the awful heat that was generated by three of them ranged alongside the bed. Both he and I were extremely uncomfortable.

The new baby was a source of great delight to all of us, although it meant that now I rarely left the island. I was feeding her myself and it was almost impossible to get to Guernsey and back between feeds. This didn't bother me at all and if anything I was glad of an excuse to stay exclusively on the island. Now that I could order my provisions on the telephone so that they came across on the next boat, there seemed little reason to go, and, strangely, I felt that the less I left the island the less I wanted to.

That second winter on the island was an exceptionally rough one. Possibly living well inland as we had done all our lives we were still unused to the sight and sound of a wind that could rock the trees to their roots, litter the paths with huge branches and sweep the sea-green over the harbour wall, leaving a trail of stones and seaweed in its wake.

Looking back it seems to us that the gales we had those early winters were of a strength and ferocity that we rarely see these days—unless, as I say, we have grown accustomed to them now.

Certain is that after one exceptionally wild night we

49

discovered next morning that two pinnacles of rock known as the Bishops, which stood in a small inlet on the west coast towards the south point had crashed down. Another gale accounted for a large and spectacular natural arch of rock which formed the seaward boundary of a huge Creux or hole at the south end. I thought ruefully of my

> island valley of Avilion;
> Where falls not hail, or rain, or any snow,
> Nor ever wind blows loudly . . .

It knew how to blow loudly here all right!

8

Alarms and Excursions

Tranquil as our life is for the most part, we undoubtedly see our share of drama from time to time, and our neighbour isle of Jethou has been responsible for this on more than one occasion. One day, after we had been living in Herm for a few years, Peter and I were setting off for Guernsey when we heard the bell on the Jethou landing pealing. This was supposed to be an emergency signal to summon help from Herm, and to be used only in the event of dire need, as Jethou had no boat and no telephone. However, the then tenants had so abused this arrangement, calling the Herm boat over on occasions when the 'emergency' was no graver than that they had run out of cigarettes or, more usually, drink, that we had come to regard the ringing of the bell as no more than a nuisance. On this particular occasion Peter had an important appointment in Guernsey, for which he was already running late, so that when the bell sounded as we passed within sight and sound of the island it was a case of "Wolf, Wolf" and Peter gave the order to the skipper to carry straight on for Guernsey. Glancing back at the island as we passed I saw a figure wading out into the water and making frantic efforts to attract our attention. She seemed more than usually agitated, and on calling Peter's attention to her he decided to put in at the little slipway after all. As we came within earshot we saw that it was the elderly retainer of the island, and she called out, "Get a Doctor quickly there's been an accident." More she wouldn't say, so we put back to Herm as quickly as possible and Peter got through on our newly established telephone to

51

the doctor. The doctor was also inclined to treat the matter lightly, as he said he had twice recently been summoned to the island, only to find on arrival that his 'patient', far from being seriously ill had merely over dined and wined and he had wasted much valuable time which he could ill afford. However, we managed to persuade him that on this occasion it did appear to be a genuine emergency, so he promised to attend. On arrival at Jethou he discovered that there had been a shooting accident and the tenant of the island had been shot through the head. He was unconscious, but still alive, and he was rushed to hospital in Guernsey and operated on and his life miraculously saved, although the bullet had passed right through his head, destroying that part of the brain controlling his memory, so that on recovery he had no recollection of anything at all prior to the accident.

The tenancy passed fairly soon afterwards into other hands and we never saw either of them again.

For a while the island enjoyed a more serene existence, but then it passed into the hands of tenants who once again provided us with plenty of alarms and excursions. One night we realised that there had been no lights showing from Jethou for the past two nights, which seemed rather strange as we knew that the tenant was away but that his wife was still on the island. Peter resolved to investigate next morning. He was a little loth to land as a large and very fierce boxer dog was kept on the island—indeed, he had been known to attack one of the local boatmen who had landed on the island, getting hold of him by his leg and shaking him as if he weighed no more than a rabbit. Peter, therefore, contented himself by sailing close inshore around the island and shouting loudly to see if he could raise anybody. Not a sign of life anywhere. He returned to Herm and reported the matter to the police, who came across in a launch some while later and on arrival off Jethou found that the landing slip (a mechanical contrivance let down on rails into the sea) was out of action and the only way to land was to launch a rubber dinghy and make for one of the small pebbly beaches on the lee side of the island. Even here there was a considerable swell running and Peter had the diverting sight of watching three helmeted policemen bouncing about in the rubber dinghy in the waves and then, a large wave catching them, they were suddenly swept ashore and spilled out in an undignified heap on to the pebbles. They searched the island and eventually came across the tenant's wife lying in a coma behind a shed near the landing stage, where, judging by the state of her sodden clothes, she must have been for at least forty-eight hours. The dog stood guard over her and it was only with some difficulty that it was brought under control and the woman carried up to the house. Her removal to hospital had to wait until the tide had risen and the landing stage was again in operation. She recovered, and shortly afterwards left Jethou to live in England. Her husband stayed on and some months later was involved in an accident which all but cost him his life, and did indeed cause the death of another.

Setting out to visit our hotel with a friend, one calm August night their little pram dinghy, for some inexplicable reason, overturned. Unnoticed by anyone in Herm they clung on to the upturned keel. Slowly the boat drifted down the channel between the two islands, then, carried by the tide, round the south end of Herm and far out along the east coast towards the north. Early the following morning the tide turned and the dinghy with the two exhausted men still clinging to the diminutive keel was carried south again. Sometime between one and two in the morning the friend, his strength at last at an end, fell off and was drowned. By a fortunate chance a local fisherman, plying between Sark and Guernsey at about nine o'clock, noticed a dark blob in the sea some way north of his course and decided to investigate, and so came across the almost unconscious tenant of Jethou and the upturned dinghy, and brought him safely ashore after a truly miraculous escape from death.

Now, I am happy to say, Jethou is in the hands of people who live there quietly and contentedly, and without recourse to such dramatic events.

Returning home from one of my rare shopping trips to Guernsey one day in the January of 1952, just as we were going through the harbour mouth and heading out to sea, we heard the boat's name being called through the loud hailer which the watch house uses to call to craft leaving or entering the harbour. The skipper circled the boat slowly round below the watch tower.

"Is the Major aboard?" we heard.

No—but his wife is."

"Well, let me speak to her."

I stood up in the bows to listen.

"Will you tell your husband when you go ashore that there is a mine somewhere off the Herm coast. Tell him to try and get a rope round it and pull it in—it will be quite harmless. It's been in the sea since the war and the firing mechanism will be rusted up."

I promised to tell him and duly passed the message on when we arrived back in Herm. We had seen nothing of the mine on our trip across. Peter called Philip and together they went down to the harbour and peered out to sea. They also went along the coast in either direction searching. I went up the hill home. Peter came home shortly after six o'clock.

"Well," he said, "we saw your mine. It was too far out to get a rope around it and we last saw it drifting back towards the south point of Guernsey—the tide's running quite fast, it will be well out by now."

We both forgot that tides turn, and a tide running swiftly out will run as swiftly back. A little before nine o'clock we were both sitting by the fire, Peter was reading and I remember I was knitting a pale-blue cardigan for Penny. Suddenly there was the most enormous explosion. A double earsplitting crack was followed by a reverberating roar. The house literally shook and a window pane crashed on to the floor. We both acted instinctively and hurled ourselves to the ground; both my knitting needles had snapped in my hands. A moment later I ran to see if the children were all right, and Peter ran to the boiler room. We both thought the hot water boiler had blown up.

54

Astonishingly none of the children had even woken up. It was a full minute or two before we remembered the mine.

Peter donned his duffle coat, took up his hurricane lamp and hurried down the hill. There was no one to be seen in the village, but the path along from the harbour past the cottages was littered with stones from the sea bed, broken glass and tiles.

And then he saw Philip hurrying along from Rosiere and went to meet him. Together they set out to call at every cottage to see if anyone had been injured.

Miraculously no one had so much as a scratch. This was due, no doubt, to the hour as everybody was indoors. Had it exploded by day when many would have been outside, several perhaps in the harbour area, we could hardly have expected to escape casualties.

The island storeman, Stan, and his wife Betty, lived in one of the farm cottages and she had the narrowest escape. She was expecting a baby and had gone to bed early and was sitting up in bed reading when the explosion occurred. Great lumps of heavy plaster fell from the ceiling on to her bed, missing her by inches.

Days later, when we could spare the time, we went down at low tide and found where the mine had detonated. Just off the end of the harbour is a small reef of rocks, and it was here, on a rising tide and with a fresh south-westerly behind it that this wartime relic exploded. It could well have been in the sea for as long as ten years.

The point of detonation was only about 40 yards from the end of the harbour and about 100 yards from the nearest cottage. The damage it caused was enormous and, as often happens, peculiar. Windows which faced the blast were mostly intact, whilst those on walls facing away were broken, sucked out it seemed. Slate roofs stood up to the blast very well with only here and there a patch where several slates had been blasted in or sucked out, but tile roofs were completely destroyed. They seemed to have been lifted bodily several inches, or even feet, from end to end and had then dropped back asprawl and broken and the guttering hung rakishly down the sides of the building or lay on the ground below.

The roofs of the Mermaid Tavern and adjoining barn, the Mermaid Cottages and Foxglove Cottage had been so treated. Three-quarters of all windows were broken and most doors and window frames wrenched out. Glass and broken tiles, seaweed, pebbles and smashed rock from the sea bed lay everywhere. The end of the harbour which is made of massive granite blocks had obviously been moved and here and there cracks several inches wide had opened up in it.

Six hundred yards away and 300 feet higher up, the roof of one of the farm barns was beyond repair. Windows in Belvoir House in a sheltered little valley on the opposite side of the island were broken. Pieces of mine casing were later found on the roof of the manor house on top of the hill, and months later I found a piece of this same jagged metal embedded about 6 feet above the ground in a tree in our garden.

The incident did of course have its lighter side and everyone had his or her 'bomb story' to relate.

Several people had been in the Mermaid Tavern and they had a stirring tale to tell. Like Peter and I, at the first crack of the explosion they had all hurled themselves to the floor. When the last reverberation had died away they scrambled to their feet and dashed outside, and were immediately drenched with a tremendous deluge of sea water. It seemed that when the mine exploded, a vast column of water, cracked stone, beach pebbles and seaweed had been thrown up into the air. On the principle that what goes up must come down, those rushing from the inn were just in time to be at the receiving end of its descent. Fortunately, although soaked through, no one was struck by falling debris.

On the darts scoring board a squiggly line down the board showed how the scorer had flung himself to the ground still clutching the chalk. One man who had been standing at the bar still held in his hand the severed handle of a glass beer tankard, while the tankard itself stood, without a drop spilt, on the bar. The hanging lanterns from the ceiling were severed neatly at the end of their flexes and stood unbroken in a line along the bar counter.

We found on closer inspection that the damage, seemingly bad enough at first sight, was even worse than we feared and clearly well beyond our means to put right. Naturally all the buildings carried the normal fire, storm and tempest insurance cover, but damage from such a thing as a sea mine was specifically excluded. It seemed like the death blow to our hopes and plans.

The Government of Guernsey was also deeply concerned and that same morning saw a representative body of officials stepping ashore to assess the damage. To our intense relief they agreed to shoulder the burden of the cost of the extensive repairs so that our anxiety, though very real at the time, was happily short lived.

In the event, and many months later, we were able to reflect on how sweet were the uses of adversity, in that we now had several brand new and stalwart roofs, window frames and doors to replace many that had been in poor shape before the near catastrophe.

9

The Community Grows

One day Philip came to us brandishing a letter and gave it to us to read. It was from a friend of his, Mick, who with his wife Bunty and three children was living in Wiltshire and running a small antique and gift shop. He wrote to ask what chance there was of joining us on the island. The life we led, he wrote, was just the sort of thing he had dreamed about and described how he had written day-dreaming letters to Bunty from beleaguered Malta during the war, visualising a cottage by the sea and the simple 'away from it all' life.

We talked it over and decided that the time was ripe for developing the tiny little gift shop that existed down in the village by the harbour and which did a somewhat halfhearted trade in postcards and souvenirs. Mick was probably just the man to do it. Moreover, the thought of having three more young children on the island was a very stimulating one, and it didn't take us long to decide to ask Mick and Bunty to join us. They arrived one cold February day and any romantic

58

dreams they had cherished about island life must have vanished as they stepped ashore to see Peter, grimy and perspiring, heaving sacks of coal ashore from a fishing vessel, and on reaching the village, to witness Philip, drain rods in hand, measuring his length along the muddy ground while he attempted to free a blocked drain.

We made over one of the farm cottages to Mick and Bunty, and Mick's first weeks on the island were spent in doing it up and making it a fit habitation to live in. They asked us round about a month after they had started work on it and we were astonished to see the transformation. Still fairly unprepossessing from the outside, the cottages faced uncompromisingly north, with a dour grey stare to the hills of the common; inside, however, Mick had worked wonders, and the once ramshackle interior would now have stood favourable comparison with any conversion scheme from the pages of *Ideal Home*. Mick and Bunty were certainly home makers, and we resolved that this quality was one we must look for when adding to our community in the future.

We have softened the grey granite outside walls of the cottages over the years and now they each have a small porch and we have moved the road further back from their front doors so now each has a small garden, all of which greatly improves their appearance.

Simon was 5 years old in the winter of 1951, and since Mick and Bunty's arrival with their three young children, two of whom were twin boys of 5½ years, we began to think about schooling. The problem was happily answered for us in an unexpected way.

That Christmas Peter Scott approached Peter and said he would like to include Herm in a round-Britain broadcast to precede the Queen's speech on Christmas Day. We were very thrilled, as quite apart from the excitement of being in a broadcast ourselves, there was the gratification of knowing that Herm was to be 'put on the map' at last! Peter Scott arrived on Christmas Eve and we spent the afternoon walking around the island and showing him all we knew of it. He was delighted to find we had a large flock of Brent geese feeding on our shores. We promised to keep a tally of them for him and to notice when they arrived each year and when they left to head north for the summer, and we have done so ever since. Their numbers have grown over the years and now we have about forty to fifty pairs with us each winter. They always arrive during the last weeks of October and leave during the first weeks of April. For some days before their departure they take longer and longer flights in ever widening circles and then one day, flying in V-formation, they head firmly north and out of sight, honking a last goodbye until next year. We always feel rather sad to see them go, even though it means that warmer weather is on the way and summer not far off.

On our walk round the island that Christmas Eve, Peter Scott jotted down all the different species of birds he saw in an hour. We still have the list and it numbers twenty-three birds.

Christmas Day, a blustery, windswept one, saw Peter and I clad in duffle coats, bracing ourselves in the strong wind against the battlements on the top of the keep, clutching our microphones and talking to Peter Scott. It was a nerve-racking experience; the wind rocked the pine trees below us and whistled through the battlements, and I can remember how I had to say, "I'm sorry, I didn't hear what you said" to more than one question put to me. Our friends who heard the broadcast, however, were reassuring and said that the Herm bit had an undoubted atmosphere of windswept island life!

Early in the New Year we received a letter from an ex-school teacher, a widow, who had listened to our Christmas broadcast and had heard Peter say that one of our more immediate plans was to start a little school. Had we found a school teacher yet? And if not, might she offer her services? We were interested and replied to her letter and eventually fixed up for her to come to us.

There were now four children of school age on the island and Mrs. Stephenson was quite agreeable for Jo, now 3½, to attend as well. Mrs. Stephenson was a fine person. White-haired and elderly, she was very much one of the old régime of school marms with a firm belief in the value of the three 'Rs'. She gave them a sound basic training in these three subjects and with so much individual teaching they came along fast. Jo could read fluently by the time she was 4½. There must have been times, however, when Mrs. Stephenson's eagle eye wandered as, for instance, on the day when Jo was sent home in disgrace with shorn locks and an envelope of curl after curl of her hair clutched in one small fist. She had been discovered under her desk, busily at work with the school scissors.

Mrs. Stephenson stayed with us for two years and then the claims of an ailing sister took her back to England. It all happened rather suddenly, and in the welter of other important things to attend to the school lapsed for many months and the children ran free. With so much of interest around them, however, they were seldom at a loose end and seemed to be happily enough engaged with some ploy or other, so that we never felt that they were suffering much from the absence of any regular schooling.

10

A Question of Time

About this time we started negotiations with the Board of Administration about the drawing up of a new lease, based on the information which we had acquired through the accounts which we had been painstakingly keeping, and which only too clearly reflected the troubles and anxieties of the past three years.

Many months of work and to-ing and fro-ing between the island and Board ensued, and always we found them friendly and helpful. Eventually the terms for a new lease were set out.

It set the period of our tenancy at sixty-six years—which was slightly disappointing, as we had hoped for 99, but was nevertheless adequate, although as I pointed out, it would mean that Simon would be in his early seventies when faced with the possibility of having to leave the island. We were to have financial assistance to help us with the heavy capital burden of putting in public services, and the virtual reconstruction of some of the dilapidated buildings, and some revenue to help towards the maintenance of public services. This money was to come from the poll tax, which is a levy charged on everyone who lands on the island, and at the time stood at 1s. We were granted a loan and the money to be repaid from the poll tax. From Guernsey's point of view this was a satisfactory arrangement, as the repayment of this necessary infusion of capital came not from Guernsey Revenue, but entirely from money raised by taxes levied on Herm itself.

One aspect of the lease which did not please us overmuch

was that the rent should be on a sliding scale, so that our landlords, the States of Guernsey, shared in any profits we might make. The greater the profit, the steeper the rent we paid. This seemed to us to strike at the very roots of incentive and would without doubt have a stultifying effect on our endeavour. Moreover, we felt strongly that nothing would be achieved by putting such a curb on us, whereas if we were allowed to prosper it would immediately be reflected in the general appearance and attractiveness of the island, and would in fact be more of a recompense to Guernsey than the few pounds they might hope to skim off. It seemed, in fact, a short-sighted policy.

However, these terms were the best that we could negotiate, and the next stage was that the proposed lease should appear in the Billet d'Etat, which is a booklet circulated to all members of the States of Deliberation, and containing proposals from various States committees for their consideration before the next States meeting, so that they can acquaint themselves with the subject matter of the various items on the agenda put forward by these committees on which they will be asked to vote. The States of Deliberation sat on these proposals and Peter and I were present in the public gallery to watch and listen.

The proceedings are steeped in age-old ceremony and tradition. The States of Deliberation is composed of the Bailiff, who is the president, twelve Conseillers and thirty-two Peoples Deputies, and ten Parish representatives or Douzeniers. In addition the two law officers of the Crown, H.M. Procureur (the Attorney General) and H.M. Comptroller (the Solicitor General) have a voice in the House, but no vote. The Conseillers are usually presidents of the more important States Committees and the Peoples Deputies are elected by the People and are the equivalent of Members of Parliament in the United Kingdom.

The Deputies file in first and take seats facing each other across a central aisle. They are followed by the Conseillers who sit on a raised dais across the end of the chamber, with the Bailiff's high-backed chair in the centre. When all are

63

present they all stand up and the Bailiff enters. He enquires in French if His Excellency the Governor is 'within the precincts'. If the answer is in the affirmative, a Court servant is despatched to ask His Excellency to join the assembly. On his arrival, the Bailiff shakes hands with His Excellency, and then follows the Lord's Prayer in French, after which everyone sits down and proceeds with the business of the House. The various proposals already contained in the Billet d'Etat are put forward by the presidents of the particular committees concerned. Questions are asked, opinions expressed and the proposals are then voted on. This is not done by a show of hands, but by everyone entitled to a vote calling out for or against in French—"*Pour*" or "*Contre*". A count is taken if there seems to be no disparity in the volume of sound from the 'for's or 'against's.

There were several projects before the one in which we were concerned, but eventually our turn came and the President of the Board of Administration presented the Court with the substance of the proposed lease. One or two questions were asked and answered, and then to our shocked astonishment and to the evident surprise of the Board, H.M. Comptroller stood up and said that he couldn't recommend the House to approve an arrangement which envisaged the States agreeing to assist with the revenue costs of public services for so long a period as sixty-six years, and he therefore proposed that there be a seven-year break clause in the lease, thus reducing the effective length of the lease from our anticipated sixty-six years to seven. Our astonishment was the greater because H.M. Procureur had sat in on all, or most of, the meetings with the board during which the proposals had been drawn up and had given no indication that he would speak against them. His surprise tactics paid off, and before the board could muster its defence on our behalf the amended proposals with the seven-year break clause were approved and passed by the House.

All that remained was for both parties to sign the lease. We wriggled and squirmed and held off signing for a year, whilst we fought for better terms, but were unsuccessful and finally we signed. The board with whom we had, and have always enjoyed friendly and sympathetic relations, assured us that the chances of the break clause being invoked were negligible; we knew this to be so but were not to be comforted. We knew equally certainly that, without any security of tenure beyond seven years, if we wished to raise capital at any time to develop our business we would not be able to do so. Moreover, hateful as it was to consider, in the event of Peter's death and my consequent inability to carry on by myself, I would be left with most of my capital tied up in the island, and a lease of no value whatsoever to sell. We had set up our stall with the clear understanding that the lease would be a lengthy one and had already invested enough of our own capital to be placed in a very dangerous position by curtailment of the lease period. Not to mention the fact that we had come to Herm, in our own minds at any rate, to make our home there, put our roots down and settle down for the rest of our lives. The very ground seemed to rock beneath our feet, we pleaded for a change of heart about the break clause, but to no avail, and at last we capitulated—because we had to have a lease of some kind.

11

Benjamin

Our next child, Benjamin, was born in the summer of 1952, another long, hot summer, and I can remember in the last weeks before he was born how I used to trail wearily up and down the hill. Even the children found the heat hard to bear and Jo and Penny would take it in turns to let Sapper help them up the hill. He was a long-suffering dog and would stand still and wait until one of them had him firmly by the tail and then he would plod steadily upwards, trailing his young 'hanger-on'. If, however, Simon, older and according to Sapper, quite capable of walking up by himself, tried to hitch a lift he would stand quite still, gazing stolidly ahead and refuse to budge.

Ben was born in July in the mid-morning of a hot summer's day and this time the sea was like a shimmering, placid millpond when the doctor came across and all went smoothly and easily. It was nice to have another baby and a second boy in the house.

The following winter we set about some very necessary alterations to the house. The kitchen was already much too small for us; we used it as a dining-room as well and we were impossibly cramped. We planned to extend it forward over the flat roof of the larder below.

It was inevitable that any building we did be done in the autumn and winter, as everyone on the island was far too busy during the summer season, quite apart from our wish not to spoil the tranquil and peaceful atmosphere of the island for our summer visitors by the grind and clatter of concrete mixers and building operations in general. But this did mean that whenever we did put any work in hand we seemed to be constantly at war with the elements. And so it was on this occasion; no sooner had we got the west and north walls of the kitchen opened up than the equinoctial gales were upon us and work—and, for that matter, living—was carried on under appalling conditions. The rain poured down, the wind lashed and ripped at the tarpaulins and water streamed in across the kitchen floor. We had hoped to be able to continue to use the far end of the kitchen whilst the work went on as, however gutted the kitchen was to become, we had perforce to keep the solid-fuel cooker going to supply the house with hot water; but it was quite impossible. We would have been more comfortable bivouacking on the North Pole.

We decamped as far as cooking and eating was concerned to the ramshackle building next door, a part of the manor house which was high on our list for demolition as soon as we could get around to it. We cleaned it up as best we could and installed a small bottle-gas stove in a little room which appeared to have been a washhouse at some time, as its only furnishing was a huge stone sink.

For the next two months we cooked and ate our meals there, darting from one building to the other, frequently in pouring rain, across an increasingly muddy yard and carrying the younger ones swathed in macs. Always at six in the evenings the children ate over there and then went back to the house and smartly to bed. Peter and I then repaired to the drawing-room and its open fire in what was left of the house for what we always felt to be one of the most rewarding moments of each day. With the children in bed and the island as it were 'safely battened down' for the night, we had our evening drink and either talked or didn't. The day's events, tomorrow's requirements, the children, the farm, the boat, the building work. The state of our bank account, the problems and responsibilities, the worries and the satisfactions. The pattern was by then, well established and we still keep to it today, over twenty years later.

I remember that autumn especially well because of the household difficulties and because it was so exceptionally turbulent. I remember how occasionally, our evening drink over and well wrapped-up against the slanting rain we would return to our shell of a kitchen and, opening up the fire door of the cooker, would grill steaks over the glowing coals. Sitting there on packing cases with two walls opened up to the elements, the roar of a pressure hurricane lamp and the howling of the wind through the lashing trees as orchestral accompaniment, we would eat our steak with a glass of red wine and felt that for atmosphere our surroundings couldn't have been surpassed by any grand dining-room in the world!

At last the work was completed and we were able to move back into our much improved kitchen-living-room. In addition to doubling the floor space we had replaced the old small-paned window with a large picture window of plate-glass, with a deep elmwood sill, and it splendidly improved our view westwards to Guernsey and northwards beyond the fields of Herm across the sea to the Casquets lighthouse.

Having such an expanse of sea and sky to watch we began to be conscious of things of which we had been quite unaware when we lived in England—the distance, for instance, that the sun travelled along the western horizon between sunset in midwinter and sunset in midsummer. In midwinter we noticed that the sun set over the most southern point of Guernsey, Saint Martin's Point, and then as the weeks went by, the days lengthened and the sun, as it set, crept slowly along the skyline of Guernsey until by mid April it sank at a point directly opposite our house over Saint Peter Port and by midsummer day it was right over the north of Guernsey, and then began its slow journey back again. We noticed that as the sun got towards the mid point of its journey in either direction it appeared to accelerate over the central section.

I began to be adroit at interpreting weather signs. I learnt to tell at a glance if rain approached and could estimate to within a minute or two how long before the shower reached us, and often how long the rain would last. Very useful when washing was out on the line! I learnt to tell the direction of the wind and to assess its strength and to judge the temper of the sea to understand its moods according to which wind blew.

ormer shell

dog whelk

Pennie

12

"What do you do in the Winter?"

One of the first problems we had to face up to in Herm was how to keep employed during the winter months those of our staff who were engaged primarily for summer activities. Both Peter and I felt strongly that if we were going to live a normal and satisfying life on the island there must be other families living here doing the same thing, taking their living out of the island, educating their children here, in all respects living a balanced community life. This did create a problem. There would be a large outgoing of wages throughout the winter with little or nothing coming in.

We thought of the shells which were to be found in such profusion on the beaches and wondered if it would be possible to employ these in a commercial enterprise of some kind. We decided to talk to Bunty. Bunty was artistic and we were sure that if there was any potential in the shells she was the one most likely to discover it.

We helped her to collect many different kinds, and a

painstaking and back-aching job it was, involving many hours of crawling around on hands and knees searching for particular species. Later we learnt that some wind and tide conditions were more favourable to shell collection than others; we learnt to recognise a cowrie tide, when these tiny pink curled shells would lie in drifts on the beach, or a limpet tide which would produce little hillocks of shells in certain places along the tide line. Sometimes these tides would coincide with a biting easterly wind and then it was a gruelling task indeed to take advantage of them and to collect for even a short while.

Peter went to London and made an exhaustive search for glues and varnishes which would not be affected by the chemical make up of the shells. We were anxious not to produce anything that could be branded as garish or gaudy, but we needn't have worried. A week or two later Bunty brought us her first essays to see. We were astounded. It seemed impossible that she could have made the delightful little figures that she showed us entirely from shells.

There was a little crinoline gowned lady, her skirt caught up with pink rosebuds, a 3-inch-high figure of Nell Gwynne, a basket of oranges held lightly under one slim white arm, the other daintily lifting her skirt to show a trim foot and ankle. One figurine that particularly delighted us was an elegant Edwardian lady with furled parasol in her hand, and on her head a wide-brimmed swirl of hat. They were exquisite.

But only Bunty had the skill and artistry to make them and we wanted to employ as many other people as possible. Bunty showed us how even the unskilled could make attractive necklaces and brooches, and we decided to go into production.

Work was done in the various island homes and most families were involved in shell-working those early years. Even those housewives who, like myself, had young children to care for and meals to prepare, found time to work at it in the long winter evenings. By the following summer we had a considerable stock to sell.

Mick had spent the winter converting an old granite boat

71

store down by the harbour into new premises for the gift shop. He had made an attractive counter from beer barrels and drift wood from the beaches and lit it by two large ship's lanterns, one red, one green, and which were believed to be the port and starboard lights from Lord Perry's yacht *Laranda*, which he had kept in Herm during his tenancy. We were very pleased with the new shop—and so it seemed were visitors to the island—and we proceeded to do quite a lively trade with the little shell figures and jewellery, representing, as they did, island-made souvenirs.

13

Doctor on Call

The autumn of 1952 was another very wild one, when once again we had occasion to experience what the equinoctial gales really meant, day after day high winds lashed the island.

We had been having a small dinner party one evening for a couple who had recently come to live on the island. As we saw them off, well sou'westered against the rain which lashed down, driven by a gale-force wind, I remarked that I was sorry for anyone on the sea that night. As we turned back into the house and secured the door against the rising wind, I heard Penny whimper in her sleep.

I went to settle her down and, apart from feeling a bit hot, she seemed to be all right. I turned back one of her blankets and rejoined Peter in the drawing-room. Half an hour later she was crying in earnest and seemed unwell. I took her temperature; it was up but not greatly so, but within the next half hour her condition grew quickly worse, until by midnight her temperature had risen to 104 degrees and she was clearly delirious.

Thoroughly alarmed Peter telephoned our doctor. The doctor made no demur about setting out on such a night and within a remarkably short time had put out to sea with a trained Saint John Ambulance crew in the marine ambulance the *Flying Christine*. This is a high-speed launch equipped with many medical aids. It was no kind of sea for such a craft and they had a terrible trip.

Nevertheless, within forty-five minutes of first calling for his assistance, the doctor walked into our house. He diagnosed an acute infection of the middle ear and decided that Penny must be moved into hospital. On such a night it was a problem how to keep her warm enough on the journey back, and after some thought we solved the problem by means of the nursery fire-guard. We padded it with pillows and then placed her in it and wrapped her round and round with many layers of blanket and she was then carried down the hill and into the launch. Philip decided to join the crew for the return journey. Now the *Flying Christine* was battling against a full south-westerly gale. Twice momentarily she lay hove to until the coxswain saw his way through the breaking rollers, and although the sea swept green over time and again, by two o'clock Penny was tucked up in bed in hospital in Guernsey and receiving treatment to which, happily, she speedily responded.

It had been a frightening experience and yet, in retrospect, it was strangely reassuring. In spite of the frightful weather conditions a patient had been fetched and admitted to hospital within a space of two hours from first calling the doctor, a speed which could hardly have been bettered even if we had lived on the mainland.

Since then there have been several occasions when the *Flying Christine* has come across to meet some medical emergency, and we count ourselves very fortunate to be able to call on such a wonderful service.

Only once again was the weather as bad as on that first occasion, and this time the patient, was myself, suffering from an acute back ailment. A strong easterly gale was blowing directly into Saint Peter Port and the conditions in the harbour mouth were appalling. Only a lifeboat could leave the harbour. The R.N.L.I. lifeboat, *Euphrosyne Kendal*, was alerted, and with the doctor aboard she inched her way, almost submerged, into the teeth of the gale, through the Pier Heads, and so to Herm.

The discomfort of my condition and anxiety for speedy treatment in hospital kept me from worrying too much about the roughness of the sea, but I do remember what a handsome vessel it was—she was very new at the time and this was one of the first occasions it had put to sea.

About this time it became clear that the *Celia* was coming to the end of her serviceable days and we looked out for another boat. Eventually we bought the *Arrowhead*. She was smaller than the *Celia*, being only 37 feet long and with no deck space. An ex-Admiralty harbour launch, built in Bideford in 1945, we considered she was ideal for the carrying of both island stores and passengers. For large cargo loads we would need to charter a bigger fishing boat.

We painted her a gay cherry-red and picked out her name in white. She looked marvellous against the blue-green water. Most boats were white in those days—though occasionally one saw a blue or a green fishing boat—and we like to think that *Arrowhead* was the forerunner of the many gaily coloured craft we see around these waters today. Certainly she created a lot of comment at the time and she became a familiar sight on her daily trip to and from the island. From our point of view her colour proved useful in being able to pick her out easily from other boats even at quite a long distance, so that we could say with confidence, "*Arrowhead's on her way.*"

We thought we would try our hand at lobster fishing. We bought a lot of pots and told ourselves that we would soon be making a lucrative sideline quite apart from being able to keep the hotel stocked up with fresh lobsters.

Peter and I went out with the boat and helped to sink the pots, but it wasn't long before I was feeling dreadfully

75

ill. The smell of the bait and the slow roll and heave as we circled slowly around or lay stationary while the pots were dropped over the side was altogether more than I could bear. It was very different from the straight pitch and toss of a normal crossing from Herm to Guernsey and to which I was now well accustomed. I vowed I'd never go on a similar exercise again, and I never did—I never had the chance. Next day and before we'd even pulled up any of the pots a great storm blew up and swept them all away. Thirty pounds' worth of lobster pots lost overnight. We never tried again. We still have fresh lobsters in the hotel but we buy them from the Guernsey fishermen who bring them directly into our own harbour.

14

Moil and Toil

It was during the winter of 1953 that we installed a new electric light plant and this was powerful enough to enable us to have electric light all over the island. It was a long business having all the wiring put in, but at last the day came when Peter walked into the house, placed his hand on the wall switch, and flooded the house with light. Unbelievable to think we could put away the oil lamps and that I had polished my last lamp glass! It was a long time before we lost that deep glow of satisfaction that came from merely switching on the light.

We began, not before time, to direct a more critical eye at the hotel and realised that, by altering the layout of the entire ground floor, it could be operated in a much more efficient manner. The kitchen was much too small, so was the dining-room, whereas the bar seemed to us to be unnecessarily large and uncosy. At the rear of the hotel, and adjacent to the large bar, stretched a hugh barn of a build ing which prior to our arrival had been intended as a restaurant for casual trade, but had never really got going. We decided to turn the ground floor back to front as it were, house the kitchen in the old restaurant, and turn the large bar into the dining-room, this would free the dining-room for a lounge, and we would be able to convert the old kitchen into a small snug bar.

Accordingly, as soon as the last guests had left in the early autumn we started work. The place looked a shambles for month after month, and dust, plaster and rubble was every-where; but with the turn of the year, order began to appear out of chaos, and by February I was able to go over to Guernsey and chose new curtaining and furnishings for the altered rooms. I chose bright bright cherry-red covers for the chairs and a deep-blue carpet for that part of the floor which was not parquet flooring. We painted the walls and doors glossy white, and the effect, as we had hoped, was gay and crisp.

Staffing the hotel in those early years was always a source of anxiety to us, and we lived from season to season, getting together what staff we could, never sure until the season was well under way, just how successful we had been.

Lacking a trained manager, Peter contrived to keep a watching brief on the situation himself, with the help of an assistant manager or manageress, but there was constant change, and with so much else to see to, it was a responsibility he was anxious to shelve as soon as we could find a suitable manager. Indeed, so great was the pressure on Peter in those early years, and the seemingly unending run of problems and crises associated with the hotel, that we seriously discussed sub-leasing the premises and freeing ourselves from what we both considered was a tremendous burden. However, we continued and, the business being mercifully seasonal, somehow managed to struggle through to the end of September each year, when we could get our breath back, and recuperate our strength for the next year's effort beginnning in April.

One of the early staff in the hotel, I remember, was a chef, an ebullient Frenchman called Julian, who was like the small girl in the nursery rhyme—when he was good he was very very good, but when he was bad he was horrid. His cooking was superb, but his temperament was hard to live with. Not that he was bad tempered, but he was gay and full of *joie de vivre* one moment, and cast into the depths of despair the next.

I remember one occasion when the French Ambassador to the Court of Saint James's, Monsieur Massigli and his wife were due to come to lunch on the island, together with a number of Guernsey officials. Julian was highly delighted at the thought of the island being visited by his illustrious fellow countryman and was determined to do of his best. The menu was decided upon, and printed with the crossed flags of Guernsey and France adorning the cover.

Peter and Julian with the whole of the kitchen staff toiled most of the previous night, preparing the banquet. It was the first of its kind that we had ever done, and Peter was most anxious that all should go well. Then when all was prepared, and within a couple of hours of the guests' arrival the storm clouds gathered, a fresh wind blew up, and it began to rain torrentially. The lunch was summarily cancelled from Guernsey. We were dreadfully disappointed, but Julian was distraught. He seized the huge knife with which it had been intended to cut the magnificent gateau, and hacked it wildly to pieces, then held it poised dramatically above his breast, declaring that he had no longer anything to live for. He was with some difficulty placated, but it left a bitterness in his heart, from which, during the rest of his time with us, he never really recovered.

The vagaries of the weather in this sort of respect was something from which we always continued to suffer. Dinner parties or lunch parties would be booked, catered for, only to be cancelled at the last moment, due to worsening weather conditions, and we began to realise that to depend to any degree at all on outside custom for business for the hotel was completely unrealistic. The hotel would have to be large enough to operate successfully on its resident population.

We began to see where we could increase the scope of the hotel, and over the years converted several nearby cottages in the village area into subsidiary hotel accommodation. It was a successful move, and we found that far from being unpopular, many of these 'outside' rooms became much sought after, and guests enjoyed having their own little suite detached from the main building, and regarded the few minutes' walk to the dining-room and lounges as a pleasant exertion, rather than any hardship.

There was amongst the dining-room staff of the hotel one year a young Austrian named Ernst. Serious-faced and diligent, he impressed us from the start with his courteous bearing, and we were pleased when, at the end of the season, he asked if he might return again the next year. He did so, and brought with him an Austrian bride, Greta, as industrious and pleasant as himself. We promoted him to being head waiter and put Greta in charge of the chamber-maids, and were delighted when, at the end of the season, they asked if they might stay on and make a home for themselves on the island. We had no cottage available for them at that time, but they cheerfully set up house in a couple of rooms adjacent to the hotel.

Ernst put away his waiter's attire, and donning old trousers and a 'Guernsey'—a heavy, high-necked fishermen's sweater—set to on the ever-present task of winter mainten-ance, which included the conversion of a cottage to his own needs. Greta, an expert needlewoman, was an invaluable asset in overhauling the hotel linen and soft furnishings. Now, for the first time we felt that we had a hardy nucleus of reliable help in the hotel.

Dating from this time we began to turn to Austria for the staffing of the hotel, and it became the custom for Ernst to return to Austria for a few weeks each winter to recruit the various staff members we required. The system worked well, and was in operation up until very recently, when we regretfully said goodbye to Ernst when he and Greta left us to run their own hotel in England.

Today the hotel accommodates one hundred people, and we have tried, and I think succeeded in giving it a country-house atmosphere, where guests have a chance to relax and wind down from the pressures which beset them in their business lives.

An island holiday, especially an island encompassing no more than three-quarters of a square mile is by the very nature of things, a prescribed one, but this is the very reason for its restfulness. Here there are no compulsions, no sight-seeing tours that must be included in one's schedule, no museum that must be seen, no cathedral that must be visited. Every stone can be left unturned without that slightly guilty feeling that perhaps one hadn't exerted oneself as much as one should have done.

Guests who may have wondered what they would find to do on a small island, find themselves developing an interest in the day-to-day activities that go on around them—the arrival of the morning boat from Guernsey; the tractor, shaking its way down the hill, laden with milk churns, and their transfer on to the boat; the unloading of the morning cargo, always a fascinating assortment of items, which like the song in *Free as Air* might well include "A hammer and a chopper and a bottle with a stopper", or a large cargo, as when our two bulls were shipped over in loose boxes and craned ashore.

The occasions when the old crane swings into action are rarely achieved without an interested gallery of spectators, and no wonder because it must be one of the oldest cranes still in use. A rusting plate on its side records that, like myself, it is of Yorkshire ancestry and was manufactured by Bray, Waddlington & Co., New Dock Works, Leeds. Peter has an old photograph, taken well over one hundred years ago, showing the same crane standing where it does today. It is an old railway crane, mounted on a wooden trolley which used to run up and down rails the length of the quay. It was undoubtedly used throughout Herm's industrial heyday when thousands of tons of granite were shipped to England.

The guests become interested in the farm in all its aspects: the cows making their leisurely way to pasture, the milking parlour, haymaking and watching the new-born calves staggering round the fields on their uncertain legs. They make friends with the island residents, and look forward to seeing them again year after year. The various island projects are followed with an almost proprietory interest, and frequently the first words spoken by a returning guest as he steps off the boat will be, "What have you been up to this last winter. What is there new to see?" Then there will be a tour of inspection to see if they approve—which, I'm happy to say, they usually do.

15

Island Industries

Pleased with our success with the shellware, the next autumn we considered whether we could start yet another island craft.

We were anxious to produce things which, because of their rough island quality, would have an appeal over the mass-produced merchandise you could buy in the shops. We thought of weaving, and wondered if Stan, then our store-man, was the man to do it.

Stan and Betty, the land girl, had met on the island. They left and were married but had later returned to live in one of the farm cottages. He had certain artistic qualities, was fond of painting and sketching, and had a good eye for colour. We decided to let him see what he could do with weaving as a winter occupation.

We bought a large frame loom and installed it in one of the two bedrooms in his cottage where the light was good and which would make an admirable work room. We bought a quantity of wool and an instruction manual and Peter and Stan went to work. Together they threaded up the loom.

Peter studied the problem of what to do with the long length of warp and the difficulty of obtaining an even tension, and invented a huge reel from which it could be released evenly on to the loom, only to find later, as with several more of his 'inventions', that it was already standard practice in most weaving mills in England.

We were very excited about the first lengths of material that Stan produced. We liked its homespun quality and the variety and range of the colours he had employed. We decided to produce only headsquares, scarves and stoles which we hoped would have a ready sale. We had some little silk labels made for us in London, reading "Herm Island Cottage Craft" and affixed one to each article as it was finished.

By the end of the following spring we had a large stock. They looked wonderful when Mick displayed them in the shop, the grey granite of the walls showed them up to perfection. We were very hopeful that there would be a big demand for them. But alas! The price at which we had to sell them to make even a reasonable margin of profit fell well outside the range of most of our customers' pockets. We just did not have the market for such expensive goods.

We reduced the price so that it just covered our manu-facturing costs and over the next few years we managed to sell them, but as a business venture it was clearly not worth continuing. We sold the loom and the rest of the equipment.

That summer we converted a long barn adjacent to the Mermaid Tavern into a snack bar and this provided a much improved catering facility for the daily visitors. Stan was put in charge of it, and if it was a less artistic pursuit than that of weaving, it at least proved to be much more lucrative. We have continued with this up to the present day.

If lobster potting and weaving turned out to be disastrous, so also did our second attempt at catering on any scale for the daily visitors who came across from Guernsey.

Pleased with the success of the small-scale snack bar we decided to open a restaurant which would serve lunches and afternoon teas. After some consideration we selected a site in a little valley towards the north end of the island.

Looking back I find it hard to remember what was our reason for selecting this out-of-the-way site, apart from the fact that there was an adjacent well so that the provision of water was no great problem.

Again we constructed the main part of the building from concrete blocks which we made ourselves, and for weeks on end an ancient lorry we had inherited with the island trundled up from the sand pit we had dug near the Shell Beach, and deposited heaps of sand on the site. Peter had decided that it was unwise to take sand directly off the beach, because of its high salt content and the risk that it wouldn't combine properly with the cement. Bags of cement were shipped across from Guernsey in the *Arrowhead* and then the actual building began. When it was finished we bought kitchen equipment, cutlery and crockery and I made many tablecloths and table napkins of bright seersucker. A simple enough task to most people, but I had never been much of a needlewoman and I was struggling with the intricacies of a sewing machine for the first time. What should have been a task measured in hours took me weeks of painful endeavour.

We opened at last and awaited custom. None came—or hardly any—and we realised belatedly that we had made a costly mistake. In our effort to preserve the natural beauty of the island we had hidden it so completely and planted it so far off the beaten track that none found it or took the trouble to go there. We struggled to make a go of it for two successive seasons and then sadly dismantled it. The bracken and willowherb crept back and took swift possession again.

Something, however, had to be done if we were to maintain a balance of payments and run a successful business. It was extremely worrying.

There was no denying that Herm was a beautiful and wonderful place to live, but it was equally true that it was an enormously expensive place which ate up capital as a sponge soaks up water. Peter and I spent many wakeful nights worrying and planning how best to mobilise our assets and turn the island into a more viable venture. We decided on a less ambitious project as far as catering went.

It was obvious that the daily visitors would continue to flock to the beaches so we must take our catering to them. We erected a small wooden hut above Belvoir Bay. We settled it back against the hillside where it nestled quite comfortably and unobtrusively. We sold cups of tea and coffee and ice cream and sweets. But still the results were disappointing—certainly more people frequented it than the restaurant but even so the 100 yards or so we had placed it away from the bay itself seemed to be a deterrent—it was invisible from the actual bay and this was enough to dissuade people visiting it once they had settled down on the beach.

We decided that the next season we would flatten out a small platform right over the bay itself. We had at last learnt our lesson. It was useless to be too 'precious' about our commercialisation of the island; the island would never prosper on scenery alone. Catering must be at well placed points of vantage and there was no reason to assume that this would be automatically unsightly; we must make every effort to build attractively and realise that it was quite possible to achieve a pleasing blend of natural beauty with development where one complemented the other.

At about this time I had a letter from Pat, a wartime friend of mine. We had been together in the F.A.N.Y.s in Buckinghamshire. She was married now with two children and wearying of the run-of-the-mill way of life in St. John's Wood, she wrote to ask if we could fit them into the scheme of things in Herm. Her husband George was, she said, good with figures and, as for herself, I knew her to be cheerful, resourceful and hardworking, and both Peter and I felt they would be a grand couple to have with us. We exchanged letters and telephone conversations and it was all fixed up for them to come to us.

They arrived one spring morning. Always one to make

light of difficulties, Pat stepped from the *Arrowhead,* marshalling her two children in front of her. In one hand she had a large basket containing an aged and protesting cat, Chips, whilst from the other swung a glass bowl of furiously agitated goldfish. I was delighted to see her, impedimenta and all.

We gave George a small office down by the harbour, the building that had been our first school, and he took over the books, such as they were, and tried hard to keep us on the straight and narrow path where balance of payments and expenditure were concerned. He was a diligent and likeable man.

Pat took over the little hut at Belvoir on its new site down by the bay. We installed a small gas oven and in addition to selling the usual hut fare of sandwiches, cups of tea and coffee, ice cream and sweets, she baked batches of hot, fresh scones which were very popular with everybody.

Quite apart from the hut's success as a business, we found it a tremendous asset ourselves. We took to getting up early on summer mornings and going down to the bay for an early morning swim. Pat was usually there before us and as we ran down the last slope to the bay, the wonderful smell of baking scones rose to meet us.

The beach is heavenly at that time of the day, untrodden and clean with the sun paving a golden path across the sea, which sparkles with a myriad pinpoints of light. After our swim, in the fresh morning air, we would breakfast on boiled eggs, hot scones and honey and coffee.

Sometimes on a September morning, we would gather mushrooms on our way down through the fields, and fry them up and eat them with the eggs.

Pat's daughter Fanny and Jo became firm friends and both became passionately interested in the farm; they learnt to milk the cows and were always on hand to help at milking time. They were given a little calf each to look after themselves and, one way and another, spent most of their waking hours when not in school, in the farmyard.

One early morning as Peter and I lay in bed we became aware of a steadily increasing wail approaching from the direction of the farm. This was no ordinary cry or grizzle and we hopped out of bed and leant out of the window.

Along came Jo, cradling one arm in the other and howling mournfully. We ran downstairs and brought her in and dealt first aid to what was obviously a broken wrist. When we heard how she came by it we were thankful that her injuries were no worse.

It appeared that she had been helping to feed the cows and had climbed up into the hayloft above their stalls to push the hay down to them through the trap door in the floor. One large truss had got stuck and, without thinking, she jumped on it to free it, whereupon the obvious happened and she and the hay fell through the trap door together on to the stone floor between two startled cows.

Peter took her across to the doctor on the morning boat and she spent the next several weeks with her arm in plaster, though it did little to curtail her activities.

16

School with a Difference

At last, in the spring of 1954, we turned our minds to reopening the school.

Our population had risen until by now we had some ten families living on the island, and there were seven or eight children of school age. A strange situation existed in respect of education on Herm Island. We discovered that the island was not included in the Education Act covering Guernsey, so that in fact there was no legal obligation for any Herm child to be educated. We took our problem to the educational authorities in Guernsey and they agreed that, although in the absence of a law they had no legal obligation to provide a school, they had clearly a moral one, and they undertook to provide a teacher and the equipment, and we undertook to provide a schoolroom and to find a house for the teacher.

An advertisement was placed in an English paper, and we were surprised by the number of replies we received. It seemed as if every other school teacher in England felt that they would enjoy living on a little island teaching less than a dozen children. The applicants were short listed down to four or five, and these few came over for interview. Eventually Mrs. Maureen Corboy was selected.

Mrs. Corboy, like Mrs. Stephenson, was also a great success, but, unlike Mrs. Stephenson, her method of teaching was completely unconventional. Far from adhering to the three Rs she believed in developing a wide range of pursuits and interests in the children, many of which were well outside the normal range of primary school learning.

Peter and I during a TV programme.

Some of the milking herd and Fisherman's Cottage.

Herm Harbour, the Village and White House Hotel, Le Manoir and our house on the hill behind.

Shipping in heavy equipment on the barge prior to a building programme.

Our first boat *Celia*, heavily laden with supplies.

A rocky perch overlooking the Common at the North of the island.

Maureen and the schoolchildren hard at work in the Schoolroom.

English lessons were informal and popular. When they wrote essays, spelling and mistakes in grammar were overlooked so long as a flowing easy style was maintained.

Under this wise and unrestrictive guidance, the children's ability to express themselves in writing flourished splendidly, and has stood them in good stead ever since. Fanny entered for a national competition organised by a well-known custard firm. An essay had to be written. I forget what the subject was, but she carried off the first prize for her age group. The prize was a children's party, complete with a large hamper of food, and large iced cake, and—greatest delight of all—a conjurer! Some of the children were in Guernsey that afternoon, a Saturday, and returned on the boat bringing the conjurer over for the party, and he went into action there and then, trick following trick as we crossed the 3 miles back to Herm. None of them had ever seen a conjurer before, and never can he have had such a spellbound audience—his performance was delightfully free from the inevitable precocious child who knows exactly how it is done. To these children it was all pure magic. Benjamin solemnly watching pennies disappear, asked if he could try, whereupon, on being given a coin he flung it with a grand gesture over the side of the boat, announcing with a highly satisfied air, "There, I did it! I made the penny disappear!"—which on the face of it was pretty indisputable.

The party, held in the old manor keep with the desks pushed well to one side was a great success—and small wonder, considering it was the first real party any of them had ever been to. The party happened to fall on my birthday, so I was invited as well, and I think I enjoyed it almost as much as they did.

Maureen gave them an appreciation of good poetry and music, and they learnt to sing alone or together in an uninhibited way which was a delight to hear.

Every Christmas they performed a Nativity play which she wrote for them. It was performed in the chapel by the light of hurricane lanterns which threw long shadows over the old granite walls. It seemed a fitting place for the little play. It was easy to recapture something of the atmosphere of the first Christmas, sitting there in the old chapel, surrounded by the farm buildings, and within sight and sound of the cows in their stalls.

Much of their time was spent out of doors. They spent long hours on the farm helping with the animals or with the haymaking. Fanny, Jo and Penny became adept at milking the cows and frequently assisted or relieved the farmer at this task.

They made collections of shells, wild flowers and seaweeds, and started a school museum, into which all sorts of strange things found their way, ranging from a cannon ball to a Neolithic stone axe.

One day, playing in the soft loose sand at the top of Belvoir Bay, Simon unearthed a long bone. A passing visitor to whom he showed it suggested that it was probably that of a horse, or a cow. "Or a wallaby," suggested Simon. The visitor laughed and said that that was highly unlikely, but later on it was verified as being indeed a wallaby's leg bone. We knew that Prince Blucher had kept wallabies on the island and had had at one time as many as thirty of them. We could well imagine that, although diverting to see as they must have been, what trouble they must have caused—as impossible to confine to any part of the island as our ten donkeys had been. They died out during the 1914-18 war when the island was almost unoccupied, but the last of them was taken by a Guernsey family and lived in their garden for many years as a family pet.

Oddly enough, during the first five or six years of our time on the island, we kept getting reports from people who had had a fleeting glimpse of a strange animal. The reports usually came in towards dusk, and were of an animal the size of a large dog, with a longish tail and which disappeared into the undergrowth with a single bound. We were tempted to believe that we still had a wallaby on the island, but no one was ever able to get a long enough or close enough sighting to enable us to confirm this. Also there was the mystery of the animal droppings which Peter

Scott discovered and couldn't identify except that they were from a herbivorous animal. If indeed the animal was a wallaby, it would have had to have been about thirty years old, assuming that it was the sole remaining offspring of one of the original wallabies that had survived the 1914-18 period. We made enquiries at a zoo, and learnt that it was just faintly possible that a wallaby could live so long, but most unlikely.

On May Day the May Queen was crowned and the girls took it in turns to be the queen. The ceremony took place at the same spot every year, a lovely bluebell-covered knoll, ringed by blossoming blackthorn against a background of tall pine-trees. We christened the place May Queen and it has been so called ever since.

The children formed themselves into a Young Farmers' Club and brought out a magazine, each child contributing something, either a drawing, or an article or a poem. It was all stitched together with gaily coloured wool and it was circulated round the various families on the island, and I remember how we used to look forward to the weekly publication.

The first school with Mrs. Stephenson had been in the village down by the harbour, in the little cottage which is now the administration office. This was far too small for the number of children we now had on the island and so we moved the school up into the keep. The room was known as the Princess's Bedroom after Princess Radziwill, the sister of Prince Blucher.

It was a large lofty room with a beamed ceiling of Silesian pine and huge built-in cupboards of the same wood ranged along the walls. The roof of the keep was not, however, all that sound, and since there was a large water tank on the roof, it was difficult to repair it. When it rained Maureen spread buckets about the schoolroom floor and work went on to the steady "ping! pong!" of the drips falling into the pails.

The windows of the school looked across a small courtyard towards our house and as I worked in my kitchen

91

I could look across and see them at their desks. Similarly, they could look across and checkup on Mum.

A useful 'jungle-gym' in the form of a huge and aged pine-tree sprawled against the keep walls. Every playtime the children sought its branches and climbed and swung around it. There was a trap door in the flat roof of the keep and the older ones used to climb to the topmost branches of the tree and then spring across to the roof, down the trap door and the stairs below and out and up the tree again. This was one activity I preferred not to watch, though Maureen would sit unconcernedly on the stone steps outside the keep, occasionally calling them to order if they became too venturesome.

During this period we set about demolishing one end of the manor house and tidying up the rest of it. We removed an outside shell of shacky lean-to buildings on the east-facing side of the house and took away all the temporary partitions from inside it. It was a huge task and demanded an enormous amount of time and quite a lot of extra labour.

The children and their school were very much in the centre of all this activity, which interested them very much, and keeping them safely out of the way of the demolition work was no small job. I remember shooing a little group of them away from a highly unsafe wall which was about to collapse. They were solemnly singing a hymn which they seemed to think was appropriate, one line of which goes, "As fell thy manna down"!

Compton Mackenzie once referred to this same manor house as "The ugliest house in Europe", and we took considerable satisfaction in removing this stigma from it. We were left with quite a handsome house by the time we had finished with it and brought it back to its original size and shape, and in the future we were to put it to excellent use in the housing of summer staff.

One summer we had staying in the hotel the Chairman of the Education Committee of the West Riding County Council of Yorkshire. When he left Herm he was due to open a vast new secondary-modern school built to the latest specifications, with large plate-glass windows and airy spacious classrooms and large well-equipped playgrounds. A far cry indeed from our ancient classroom with the rain dripping through the roof and the ivy and virginia creeper pushing in at the arched windows.

He thought it would be interesting to draw a parallel, or rather contrast, between the two educational establishments in his opening speech and so wandered up to the school one morning to take notes. He arrived at break time and found the children all clustered busily around a strange object in the courtyard. A straw-stuffed sack was supported on four brooms. A waste paper basket head and a tow tail clearly indicated that it represented some animal.

"And what sort of an animal is that?" enquired the elderly gentleman courteously.

Back came the gleeful response. "It'sa cow, and we're playing artificial insemination!"

I often wonder if that little incident was incorporated into his inauguration speech.

If all this sounds as if basic learning must have suffered, it is sufficient to say that when eleven-plus came along, those that took it sailed through with ease—never, in some cases, realising that they had sat it!

17

Children and Pets

Rupert, our fifth child and third son, was born in the late autumn of 1954. He arrived in the witching hours of 31st October, and as the doctor handed him to me he remarked, "Well, there you are—a Hallowe'en baby for you!"

I looked at him and was bound to admit that he looked the part. He was a small elfin-looking little thing with small pointed ears and a fuzz of dark hair. He grew up to be a dark-eyed quick-silver child of merry temperament, always energetically engaged in some ploy or other. He was very different in many respects from his blond and blue-eyed brother Benjamin, who seemed to have absorbed something of the hot golden summer during which he was born, and was inclined to day-dream his way through life, absorbed in thoughts and schemes of his own, and with an equable, even temper that was rarely disturbed.

Soon after Rupert was born we decided to try and find someone to come and live with us to help me with both the housework and the children.

We advertised locally and drew a blank, and then when we'd almost forgotten about the advertisement we had a telephone call one evening from a girl offering her services. The voice sounded young and childlike and we were inclined to discount her offer, but she said she was living in Sark with her family and a trip to Sark was a not unattractive proposition so we said we would go over and see her the next day.

Accordingly we did so and were not surprised to find the

94

owner of the voice was a young 15-year-old girl, the eldest of four children—a child, in fact, herself.

The introductions over, Margaret rushed off to play with Simon, Jo and Penny in the garden, leaving Peter and me to discuss her merits with her parents. They seemed as a family to have lived a chequered life, moving around from place to place. The father was an invalid and they were considering moving back to England, but Margaret loved the Channel Islands and wanted to stay. She was, they assured us, very domesticated. We doubted it but liked her friendliness, high spirits and charm, and the children clearly got along with her exceedingly well.

When they all came in for tea half an hour later, they seemed to have decided the issue between them: the children wanted Margaret and Margaret wanted to come to the children, there was little left to be said except arrange to send the *Arrowhead* to bring her across to us in a couple of days' time.

And that was the start of a relationship which grew stronger and dearer to us over the years.

Her father died some months afterwards and her mother returned to England to live with her younger sisters and brother. Margaret adopted us as her family and made her home with us.

She was a dubious asset as a mother's help to start with as she was wildly untidy and inclined to be scatterbrained, but she showed a real flair for cookery and loved nothing better than to be let loose in the kitchen. The speed with which she could produce an airy-fairy sponge cake or batch of scones was most impressive. Nothing was ever too much trouble for Margaret, especially if the doing of it gave anybody else pleasure, and though at times she led the children into such hare-brained scrapes that our patience was sorely tried, she was a warm hearted, generous child and we came to love her dearly and wouldn't have parted with her for the world.

After Margaret's arrival it became imperative to do something about extending the house to provide ourselves with more bedrooms. We planned a one-storey extension wing to one side of the house, overlooking the walled garden and facing due south, giving each of the children their own small room and a bathroom between them.

For the lower part of the walls we used concrete blocks which were made on the island and later rough cast over the plaster. From the window-sill level upwards the walls were of vertical planks of Silesian pine, cut from a number of large beams taken from the demolished wing of the manor house next door.

The children had a fine time while this work was in progress, and whenever they were not in school they raced to see how the work was progressing. The workmen must have been sorely handicapped by their interest.

On more than one occasion one child or other would be missing when the others trooped back into school after break and Maureen, glancing out of the window and seeing him or her blissfully slapping on cement would remark, "Ah well, there's more ways than one of cooking eggs. He'll probably learn as much of value out there this morning as he will in here!" She was always tolerant and capable of encouraging interest in even the most bizarre pursuits.

Some years later we had a naturalist on the island who was making a study of—of all things—fleas, and the school children used to accompany him and watch him at work catching rabbits whence he obtained the fleas. I was not too keen on the children being present at this activity but Rupert set my mind at rest. "You know, I don't think the fleas would *want* to live even on *me*. They much prefer to live on rabbits!"

Penny, unbeknown to me, contracted to take on a pet rabbit from one of the workmen engaged on the construction of our bedroom wing who wanted to find a home for it. Peter remonstrated with her, "Penny, you mustn't do this sort of thing without asking my permission. How do you know I want a ropey old rabbit living in the garden?"

The name stuck and Ropey he became. He grew to be the largest rabbit we'd ever seen. Snow white, he stood at

96

least 3 feet high on his hind legs. He came to terms with Sapper and would follow Penny about the garden and even into the house, as companionable as any dog.

Tragically, his very friendliness was the means of his sudden end. He ran trustingly to meet a maurauding bull terrier one day and was killed instantly. It was terrible.

The children gave him a state funeral and notices were sent out to all the island families. There was a large attendance. One hotel guest who happened to turn up left dabbing her eyes and murmuring, "Oh dear! I was deeply moved!"

Next day to take her mind off the sad business I arrived back from Guernsey with a white mouse for Penny. It was an accredited male, I was assured, so it was with some dismay that a couple of weeks later Peter and I received the news that "Matthew had babies!"

And so indeed he had—we changed his name to Matilda and set about housing her offspring. And that was the start of quite an era of mousekeeping in Herm.

As each litter was born—and anyone who has kept mice will know just how frequently *that* happens—another family on the island became mousekeepers, and parents began to demur. The children hit on an idea. "Let's form a mouse club," they suggested.

Peter gave them the use of a disused room under the keep and it was soon lined with an odd assortment of mouse cages, from smart green or blue metal ones complete with every mod. con. of swings and wheels and ladders to home-made ones, converted from a tea chest or orange box or even, in one case, a doll's house. Anyone who visited the club had a job to get out again without having had a mouse foisted on to him or her, and indeed, His Excellency the Lieutenant Governor of Guernsey, over for a day's pheasant shooting with Peter, left in the evening with at least four in his pockets—"A present for your grand-children, Your Excellency!"

There seemed to be no logical conclusion to the mouse club until one day one of the children was given a couple of guinea-pigs as a birthday present. Then allegiance began to waver. Gradually the nature of the club changed, guinea-pigs took the place of mice and the mice, I suspect, were turned loose. Their breeding activities without doubt continued unabated because for many years we would come across white and piebald mice in many parts of the island.

18

Water Divining

During the autumn of 1954 we decided that, with Herm's growing population and the increasing number of visitors we were getting through the summer months, we must add to our water supply and dig another well.

Peter arranged for a water diviner to come to see if he could tell us where the well should be dug. It was fascinating watching him at work. I had always been rather sceptical until then that water diviners really possessed these strange powers, but there it was for all to see, the uncontrollable twisting, bending action of the hazel twig when he walked over a hidden source of water, be it an already-laid water pipe or a yet undetected spring. Several of us tried also and one girl living on the island at the time discovered that she also possessed this strange gift—but it was of little practical use without the additional knowledge that could decide how far down the water source was and what the yield would be.

The diviner made an exhaustive search about the island

and found several sources of water, but it was interesting that he eventually pronounced on a spot for the well that confirmed what Philip had suspected during our first summer on the island. He had noticed that in spite of the long drought, there was a persistently green, damp patch of grass in Pan Meadow.

To make assurance doubly sure we also consulted a firm of water engineers from Guernsey and, although they agreed on broad principles that Pan Meadow was the best source of water, they decided that the actual site of the well should be 50 yards higher up the hillside. The well was dug on this site, but to our great disappointment, was not particularly productive. The diviner had been right after all, and a year or two later we found it necessary to dig another well in the bottom of the valley at the site chosen by the diviner. This well is 50 feet deep and 8 feet in diameter and now constitutes our main water supply.

In the middle of all this work we ran into winter, and an exceptionally hard winter it was. We rarely have snow on Herm, but that year we had both snow and frost.

First there was the snow which turned the island into a winter wonderland of incredible beauty. The younger children had never seen snow before and they had a wonderful time. They built snowmen, a whole line of them, marching down the garden path to the door in the wall and there they stood for weeks on end.

I had a pair of old water-skis which my brother and I had bought in France the last summer before the war. They were heavier, longer and narrower than the modern version and were made, incredibly enough, of solid mahogany. We dug them out of the barn where they had lain, collecting dust, since our arrival, and ski-ed down Valley Panto and Belvoir Field. Peter made a toboggan, so the children, one way and another, had a wonderful time, and we tried not to think of the frustrating waste of time over the well digging and all other work which had come to a standstill.

After the snow came a hard keen frost which gripped the island in an icy iron hand. Because of the normally mild winters, many of the water pipes were surface laid and these were very vulnerable to the intense cold and they froze solid. For days we had to carry water in buckets from a covered well in the farmyard. Not normally more than a few minutes' walk from the house, it seemed a long way with a brimming pail in either hand.

And after the frost, the thaw, when water poured out of the burst pipes. Little rivulets appeared everywhere and our precious water supply seemed in danger of being seriously depleted. All hands turned to the task of repairing pipes. It was almost impossible to get skilled labour from Guernsey to assist, as they were in a similar plight, and Peter and Philip and every other available man toiled long hours to put things to rights.

At last the well diggers were able to get back to work. Watching their progress one day, Peter was surprised to notice that, although they were working about 12 feet down from the surface of the ground, they were turning up vast quantities of limpet shells. He mentioned this a day or two later to an archaeological friend living in Guernsey who was at once very interested and came over to inspect it. It was, as he had suspected, a Neolithic midden—or as we should say today, a household rubbish dump. He investigated it more thoroughly and amongst the shells he found a stone axe head and various worked pieces of flint which, he said, had been used as cooking utensils.

Since that day we have seen similar evidence of middens when excavating near one or other of the houses. It is interesting to think that there are places in Herm where dwellings stand today where Neolithic men and women probably had their rough stone circle huts, and I suppose it is not impossible that some of the base stones of today's houses were first rolled into position to form foundation stones to Neolithic huts three thousand years ago.

19

T.V. Entente Cordiale

Rosemary was born in the midsummer of 1956, as with Benjamin, on a day of summer sunshine and windless sea. We felt very pleased with ourselves to have rounded off the family so neatly—three boys and three girls! She was also a sunny summer child of fair hair and blue eyes with an equable easy temperament.

Eleventh June, the day she was born, was a memorable one for us in more ways than one.

The doctor attending her birth stepped off the boat at the same time as a team of T.V. technicians and cameramen who had come to start work on a programme about the island and those of us who lived there. The programme, which was to go out in July, about three weeks later, was to consist of fifteen minutes of filmed and thirty minutes of live transmission and it was the filmed part which they had arrived to shoot on the 11th June.

Peter had a hectic morning of it, chasing between doctor and Peter Bale, the producer, bedside and camera, but nevertheless, a successful two or three days' filming was accomplished and certainly the weather co-operated magnificently. It was hot and sunny every day.

The live part of the programme was the real challenge to the B.B.C. technicians as it was the first time a live broadcast had gone out from the Channel Islands, and was indeed, I believe, the most ambitious outside T.V. programme till then attempted by the B.B.C. This required, it appeared, tremendous co-operation from Telefusion Radio de France as the programme could only be got to London via Paris, and to do this the French had to construct temporary towers within visual distance of each other from the French coast to Paris to connect into the Eurovision link. The French also wanted to broadcast the programme themselves.

A week or two after the filming had been done, a team, with Max Robertson as compère, arrived to do the live part of the programme. The B.B.C. chartered a 120-foot Fairmile which had been converted to a yacht and brought over from England £50,000-worth of T.V. gear. This included two massive generators on trailers, which were offloaded by our ancient crane and towed a few hundred yards inland, mobile cameras and hundreds of yards of heavy cable. They took over Foxglove cottage, as a control room, then the hotel, guests and all—in fact the whole island. A day or two later the scene was further enlivened by the arrival of the French television team and a state of highly technical *entente cordiale* reigned, with us, the local inhabitants who were to be 'merely players', stunned onlookers to their frenzied preparations.

The French transmission was to go out first on 14th July, the B.B.C. one the following day.

By midday on the 14th, with the broadcast due at 5 p.m., the French compère had still not arrived, so none of us, although fairly well drilled in our English parts, had the least idea what was to be expected of us, except that we were to be interviewed in French, a disconcerting enough thought in itself.

To say that a state of confusion existed is to put it mildly. Near-chaos reigned. The afternoon wore on, and still no compère. The French team were getting desperate. The last scheduled boat arrived and still he didn't come, and then—with less than one hour to spare—he suddenly materialised, a cheerful little Frenchman. Nobody knows to this day quite how he got here. There was a hectic sorting out of personnel required for interview, the swiftest possible briefing, and we were on the air to France.

I can still remember my contribution to the programme, a few monosyllabic answers to the introductory queries put to me, and then after a question or two about the children, the carefully rehearsed answer *"Excusez moi Monsieur, il me faut aller. Je suis en train de leur mettre au lit."* Whereupon I thankfully disappeared and left the brunt of the interview to be handled by Peter. I speak rather better French now since Simone has come to live on the island, but at that time it was an ordeal indeed. (Simone is our *bonne a toute faire*, and a tower of Gallic strength to us. She comes from a small village in the depths of Brittany, so Herm and its winter isolation holds no problems for her.)

Right after the broadcast they phoned through to Paris and learnt that the broadcast had been rated as 'good'. Immediately the French team rushed to the Mermaid to celebrate. And what a *cause célèbre*. The pent-up anxieties of the past forty-eight hours were released in one grand and glorious whoopee, for was it not also 14th July and Bastille Day? The celebrations lasted well into the early hours of the following day.

The B.B.C. team, with their programme still ahead of them, were in no mood to celebrate yet and found these premature jubilations very trying. There were more than a few frayed nerves before 5 p.m. on the 15th.

From our point of view, even though the interviews were in English this time, it still had its worrying moments because Max intended to include some of the children in addition to Peter and me, and, naturally, we were anxious as to how they would acquit themselves. He had selected Simon—then 10, and Benjamin, 4½, to represent the family. However, when Ben's cue to run out of the house and on set arrived, he was discovered curled up in an armchair fast asleep. Hurriedly I propelled Penny—6 years old—out of the house in his stead and she fortunately put up quite a creditable performance at short notice, although when Max asked her where she had been born—expecting, and no doubt wanting, the reply, "Here in Herm," she replied, "In Mummy's bedroom of course!"

The whole business was very exciting for all of us. Some of the shots involved the hotel and the guests accepted with great forbearance the lengths of cable stretched across the dining-room and lounge, and picked their way round huge pieces of television equipment with patient tolerance.

We had at that time been seven years on Herm and the tenor of the programme was "What was it like when you came here? What have you completed of your plans? What are you going to do in the future?" and through it all "What is it like for the families living on a lonely little island and making their homes there?"

Some years later the B.B.C. again came to us for a further half-hour programme and, picking up the threads of their earlier visit, carried on showing how we had progressed in the intervening years.

20

Pottery

Thinking about the failure of the weaving venture we realised a basic truth where island crafts were concerned. Only those enterprises would succeed where we were able to employ raw materials actually found on the island and which therefore involved no sending of money out of the island and import of materials before we could begin.

Shellware was a perfect example of an industry likely to succeed for this reason. The shells come from our own beaches and only a small amount of materials, such as glue, brooch backs and elastic, have to be imported. Equally, weaving was an example of an industry likely to fail as all the raw materials had to be purchased.

What other materials had we on the island? Studying an old map one day Peter discovered that on it were marked two or three clay pits. So our minds turned to the possibility of starting up a pottery. Peter, Philip and Mick investigated the claypits and found that we had indeed several sources of easily accessible clay.

Shortly afterwards Peter and I were in London and walking round Harrods one day we noticed some pottery which greatly appealed to us. We made enquiries as to where it had been made and by whom. We discovered that it came from the Chelsea Pottery which had been founded and was now run by a potter of great repute, David Rawnsley. We called to see him and found him to be a man of great charm and friendliness. He was at once interested in our story and was determined to be helpful. He volunteered to make a test of

106

our clay to see if it was suitable to our purposes and we arranged to have some sent to him. A few weeks later we heard from him.

It was, he told us, entirely suitable and, moreover, when fired, it emerged a most lovely warm honey shade of light golden-brown. He was enthusiastic and he offered, if we were interested, to spend the following spring and summer on the island with his wife and children and to help us to set up a pottery.

Mick was also enthusiastic and excited over the project. He had some slight experience with a potter's wheel, and felt he would like to take over the running of the pottery.

Peter, however, remembering our experiences with weaving, insisted that Mick went for a course of instruction. So away went Mick to London and took a short course with David at the Chelsea Pottery.

On his return we turned out a disused building up by the farm and repaired the roof and windows. We bought and installed a kiln and work bench. Our first potter's wheel, however, was definitely of island design. Mick had an old Indian brass gong and this was mounted on a turntable. Its upturned rim was ideal for catching the surplus clay as it flew off the wheel. He fixed an old cartwheel underneath the bench where he sat as a flywheel to keep the turntable spinning. To begin with he operated the cartwheel with his foot, but finding this hard work he decided to fix a pulley system and to use an electric motor to provide a friction drive against the cartwheel. Before he had time to order a rubber band to provide the friction drive, Peter found a rubber motor tyre washed up on the beach. Mick tried it on the wheel and it fitted perfectly. The whole construction made a perfectly workable and efficient potter's wheel.

David approved when he came down in the spring and work began.

We were all very excited by this new venture and most of us went along to try our hand at either 'throwing' or modelling, some with surprising success. Peter produced some very effective heraldic-looking little beasts which we christened

'Peter's mudlarks', but we became much too attached to them to contemplate putting them in the shop and selling them.

Mick's skill developed quickly and he and David turned out some most attractive articles. Again remembering the weaving, and how our finished products had proved to be too costly for our customers we confined ourselves to the production of small things like ashtrays, small bowls and jars, all with a retail price of under a pound.

At the end of the summer David left, leaving a well-versed Mick behind him and through the following autumn and winter he built up quite a large stock of attractive articles for sale in the shop.

But now we had a problem. The previous summer Bunty had taken over the running of the shop from Mick to free him for his work in the pottery; but it was desirable, for a variety of reasons, not least that Bunty with a family of three young children to look after found the pressure of running both shop and home too great, for Mick to return to it. We decided to advertise for a potter.

Eventually we engaged a young fellow who was quite sure he was capable of the task and he arrived with his wife and child and settled into one of the farm cottages. But within the matter of a month or two it became obvious we had made a mistake.

Besides being untidy and disorganised he had too much of an artistic temperament to permit him to be happy turning out, day after day, articles which differed little from each other. In order to work to the best advantage it was necessary to make nothing but ashtrays for day after day, then day after day of identical small bowls, and so on. He liked to experiment and wasted endless time producing a variety of articles which, though in themselves attractive, were not necessarily good selling lines, or had had too much labour put into them to allow us to sell them with a reasonable profit margin. We understood and sympathised with his attitude, yet couldn't subscribe to it.

We parted company and went in search of another potter, with much the same result.

We carried on the pottery with first one potter and then another in a vain search for one who could combine artistry and skill with a commercial approach to the task, and eventually came to the regrettable conclusion that there is no such thing as a successful one-man pottery. Our situation made it impossible for us to employ more than one man on the job as we were short of accommodation and could not afford to put over more than one of the island houses or cottages to this one business.

In pottery it seems that a potter is dedicated and skilled at one particular aspect of his trade. He enjoys and is expert at 'throwing', i.e. making the pot on the wheel, or glazing, or firing or decorating, but he rarely combines enthusiasm for all these things together.

We discovered that in most potteries we visited in England different people were employed to cover all these separate functions. This, combined with the artistic trait which prevented a man persistently and conscientiously churning out dozens of identical articles, made our problem well nigh unsurmountable. After three years of struggle and considerable financial loss, we sold the equipment and closed down the pottery.

This was the third of our ventures to fail dismally and we were very worried. We loved Herm dearly by this time—it was a wonderful place to live and to bring up our children—but it was astoundingly difficult to maintain a satisfactory income from the island. During the summer when all our livelihood depended on the business we could do with the daily visitors coming over from Guernsey, there would be days when the sea was too rough for the boats to come across and no one would come at all, so trade and income were non-existent.

We began to sleep badly and would have fits of depression and worry. Round our necks hung the heavy albatross of our overdraft at the bank and, far from improving our position, we had made it steadily worse. At night—unable to sleep we would go downstairs and drink endless cups of tea and ponder and plan and try to think of a way out of our difficulties. Fortunately for both of us our fits of depression rarely coincided, so that if one was feeling 'down' the other was always there to cheer and bolster up.

It was probably during one of these wakeful sessions that it occurred to us that a way in which, with small cost to ourselves, we could increase the summer resident population of the island, and so be more independent of the daily visitor trade, would be to develop camping. Already we had a few people, mostly Guernsey residents who came over for a week or two at a time, bringing their own tents, but there was without doubt a much larger potential among would-be campers who lacked the necessary equipment. We were unwilling to inject any capital into this development in the first instance, until we saw how it went, so we came to an arrangement with a man in Guernsey who was already running a camping business over there, to hire the tents and the equipment directly to our campers in the sure knowledge that although we made nothing out of this transaction, indirectly we would benefit as it would provide additional customers for our shops, beach cafés and restaurant.

Later, over a period of years, and as we could afford it, we bought tents and eventually took over all the hiring ourselves. We enjoy the company of the campers on the island. They are a gay, resourceful lot, many of them drawn from the ranks of professional and business men who are only too anxious to leave their cars behind them and live as unsophisticated a life as possible for a few weeks. We find ourselves of an evening paying frequent visits to Little Seagull, the field near the farm, which we have put over to their use, and joining in their barbecues, singsongs round a camp fire or an impromptu cricket match.

Little Seagull is well suited to camping, as it is protected from the prevailing wind by a sheltering pinewood, yet has a lovely view north along the sweep of the Shell Beach and its offshore islets to Alderney and the Casquets lighthouse beyond.

With the same object in mind of increasing the resident holiday population we have put over two or three farm cottages which have become vacant to the purpose of holiday

110

letting, and these have proved equally popular, allowing people to integrate themselves with the island life to an extent even greater than by staying in the hotel.

Only this last winter we turned to advantage yet another source of raw material present here on the island.

The west beaches of the island are rich in beautifully coloured stones and for a long time we had wondered whether we could use them in a similar manner to the shells. We noticed how jewel-like they appeared when the tide was in and we saw them under water, or lying in pools, but how, when high and dry on the beach their lustre departed and they appeared lifeless by comparison. We were sure that if we could find some comparatively simple way of preserving their underwater appearance we would find a ready market for them. We had already explored the possibility of polishing them with a carborundum drill but the process was lengthy and involved, and as only one stone could be done at a time, it was inevitably a costly business labour wise, and so we abandoned the idea.

Now however, we have discovered a stone polishing process which is much more practical and does not involve very much costly equipment. We have converted the small room where once the children kept their mice, and later their guinea pigs, and which has since always been known as the 'Guinea Piggery', into a workshop. The equipment for polishing the stones consists of several large polythene jars which revolve constantly, powered by a small electric motor, and which contain the stones and also water and grit. The grit has an abrasive action on the stones, and over a period of five or six weeks turns them from dull, rough pebbles into jewel-like stones of great beauty.

We mount them on gold or silver chains, brooch backs or bracelets and are finding that, like the shellware, they have great appeal.

111

21

Kay and the Bird Club

When Margaret was 18 she was accepted to train as a nurse in Jersey—an ambition she had cherished since early childhood. She continued to regard us as home and spent all her holidays with us. We wondered how she would manage to pass the necessary examinations as they came along. She had left school at 14 and had had no scholastic education since. However, we needn't have worried; her natural intelligence and her boundless enthusiasm carried her through with no difficulty at all, until as a fully-fledged and well-qualified nurse, she went out to Switzerland on her first job as the resident nurse of a large international school.

Margaret is married now and is living in America. She has a small son whom she has called Benjamin after one of her Herm 'brothers', and a daughter Jenny, named after me.

About the time Margaret left us to start nursing I had a letter out of the blue from a girl called Kay who had heard about us and who wrote asking if she could come to help me with the house and children. We accepted her offer and she came to us. She was a strange character. She had no family background and had spent her life in a succession of children's homes and institutions. As she had grown older her role had been reversed and, instead of being looked after and cared for herself, she had been trained to help the staff with the care and nursing of the children.

All her life had been spent among children and she loved them and understood them, but was uneasy and inclined to be prickly in adult society. Because of her institutional upbringing she knew nothing of family life and was little given to demonstrative displays of affection, neither did she find it easy to accept it.

She was a bonny girl with blonde wavy hair and intensely blue eyes but, almost as if she had a chip on her shoulder, would adopt a gauche, masculine form of dress, sailcloth trousers, sweaters and windcheaters and flat-heeled brogue shoes. She suffered badly from asthma and always carried an inhaler which assisted her breathing. But she was courageous and uncomplaining, and none of us realised what a struggle she had to live an even reasonably normal life.

When Kay came to Herm it was the first time she had lived in the country, but, far from feeling strange, she reacted like a plant that has been starved of water and light. She seemed to absorb it in every pore and delighted in every living thing. She had an instant rapport with every animal and bird. Especially birds. She had known nothing of them previously, but within a month or two could identify every species which came her way.

We have many bird books and all her leisure time was spent studying bird lore. We bought her a pair of binoculars for her birthday and introduced her to some ornithologists in Guernsey who taught her to ring the birds' legs with small, numbered rings so that their migratory habits could be analysed. She befriended a magpie fledgling that had fallen out of its nest and kept it in a cage in her room, feeding it almost hourly in a determination to rear it, and was successful. She called him Beauty, and as the bird

113

grew he would answer her call and fly to her from any part of the garden and perch on her shoulder.

She formed a bird club among the island children and took them out on expeditions, teaching them all she was learning herself, and gave them little prizes for diligence and enterprise. I came across a bird book recently, inscribed, "To Ben, for trying hard, with love from Kay."

Ben must have been about 6 at the time.

Penny recalls how, in order to illustrate the territorial habits of robins, with Kay's help she ringed the leg of a robin which they caught in our garden, with a red ring. Similarly, Jo ringed a robin which she caught in the Home Field, with a blue ring. Thereafter, they would look for their two robins, and Penny's robin was never seen to stray into the Home Field, and Jo's robin was never seen in the garden, although the two territories adjoined each other.

The children built hides with Kay, and they would spend hours bird watching and photographing. Sometimes one or two of them camped out with her overnight on Hermetier, a tiny little offshore islet with a thatch of grass on top, alone with the gulls and oystercatchers. They developed an interest in and knowledge of birds which has never left them.

But the bird club came to a sudden and tragic end. One day Jo ran to our room very early in the morning to say that Kay was ill and was calling for us. We hurried to her to find that she was in the throes of a very bad cardiac asthmatic attack. Peter ran to telephone the doctor, but it was too late—while Peter was still speaking to him Kay died in my arms.

Poor Kay, she had at last come to live in a home where she was loved and accepted as a member of the family and had lived only eighteen months to enjoy it. It was some consolation to know that those eighteen months had gone some way towards replacing all she had missed in her childhood.

Sapper also died that summer. He was 12 years old and a fair age for a labrador, but we all felt his loss keenly, and

114

couldn't bring ourselves to think about replacing him, for the time being at any rate.

22

Exploring the Shore

One Christmas we gave Simon the equipment for building a dinghy. We set up a work bench for him in one of the barns and all that winter he worked at building his boat. The island carpenter would help him from time to time and when, towards its completion, it was ready for sandpapering, painting and varnishing, the other children were enlisted to help.

It was months before it was finished, but at last came the day when it was carefully hoisted on to the tractor trailer and all of us followed it through the fields down the hill to Belvoir bay.

Rosemary performed the launching ceremony and wished her God speed and Simon, beaming all over his face, put to sea.

Now we were able to go on little excursions, pottering around the coast and exploring inlets and creeks we'd never seen before. Sometimes we would take a picnic and Simon would ferry us two by two to a hidden-away cove which was inaccessible except by sea and where we would spend the day swimming and lazing on the hot sunbaked rocks. It is hard to describe how wonderfully clear the water is around Herm. Leaning over the bows of the boat as it slips through the water you can see right to the bottom, even when it is quite deep. There are the upright fronds of many coloured seaweeds— golden-browns, pink and red and emerald-green—swaying in the movement of the tide, and shoals of tiny fish weaving their swift way among the fronds.

Sometimes a crab will sidle its way across the sandy sea bed, or a larger fish, a mullet or pollack, glide silently across the rock face and disappear into the dark crevice. The sun slanting through the water gives it a sparkling translucency and lights up the sea anemones on the dark rocks until they glow like a myraid richly hued jewels.

Peter, and the children as they grew older, quickly became adept at swimming with a snorkel, mask and flippers and would describe to me the thrill of discovering this new underwater world at close hand where everything seems to be just a bit larger than life and the seaweed sways about with a strangely slow-motion action; the excitement of swimming amidst a shoal of fish who, far from being shy, display a friendly curiosity and seem in no hurry to dart away. Rupert says that looking up through the water when he dives down it seems that the surface is covered with silver paper because it is so shiny and sparkling.

Peter, who once hated to swim in deep water where he knew seaweed to be, explores these depths quite happily now that he wears a mask and can see clearly, and in fact loves nothing better than to part the fronds and glide between then as he explores the underwater reaches of the cliff face.

Regrettably, I never shared their enthusiasm for this activity, much as I envied them. The moment I don a mask I get a panicky, breathless feeling which I've never managed to overcome.

One day Peter and I were entertaining to tea a keen

117

yachtsman—Simon's headmaster when later he went away to public school in England. After tea we walked about the island. As we rounded the cliff path towards Belvoir bay he asked if any of the children had learnt to sail.

"Oh yes," we replied. "Simon sails—look, there he is!"

Round the headland from Shell Bay spun his little brown dinghy. Hoisted amidships was an oar and from it billowed a scarlet bathing towel. He was making a merry pace. He looked for all the world like a picture in an old copy of Peter Pan that I have, Peter in his bird's-nest boat with his shirt for a sail.

Nevertheless, these early adventures made a useful inauguration for the real thing, when he eventually went to Bryanston and learnt to sail in Poole Harbour.

One night an unsuspected gale sprang up and the little dinghy broke away from her moorings and was dashed to pieces against the rocks. We were all very distressed, especially Simon, and Peter promised him he would replace it as soon as we could find a suitable boat.

Some months later we did find one in Guernsey. She was practically circular in shape, and roomy, stable and buoyant, and seemed to be ideal for family purposes. She had a small inboard engine, but, although we kept this in for a while, we later had her converted into a sailing dinghy. Peter and Simon sailed her across to Herm. We were on the harbour to greet them and Jo, looking at the brown, tubby craft as she came alongside, remarked, "It looks like a big fat sunburnt fisherman—Fat Sam!" And so she came by her name.

Now that we had a larger boat we were able to make bigger offshore excursions and would often visit the little islets sprinkled along the coast that are crowned with springy turf and clumps of pink sea thrift. In the spring these are covered with nesting seabirds and often we would land and, moving around quietly, we would find eggs in every stage of hatching out from the first tiny hole in the shell to the stage when the young gull struggles out.

We learnt how the embyro bird in the later stages of its

development has a tiny little white saw tooth on the upper surface of its beak and with this it literally saws the shell away to provide a big enough hole to emerge. We have watched the wet, bedraggled little thing struggle to its feet and shake itself, seen how, in a surprisingly short time, its feathers dry in the sun and air and fluff out and it takes its first uncertain steps.

It is possible to find an egg which is already showing a tiny hole, and holding it carefully, whistle into the hole— then putting it up to your ear, you can distinctly hear the unhatched gull whistle back again.

There is a tall craggy islet offshore from Belvoir called Caque Robert (pronounced Cacker Robare). It takes its name, which is old Norman French, from it resemblance to Duke Robert of Normandy's helmet. The Duke was the father of William the Conqueror and he sailed to the islands in 1033 and sought anchorage for his fleet off the north coast of Guernsey. It's exciting to think that the Duke's ships sailed these same waters—and more than probably anchored off Herm. Caque Robert stands 60 feet high and though steep it is a fairly easy scramble up it once you know the way. Often we would load up *Fat Sam* with our picnic things and sail across there, then climb to the flat top and lie in the soft grass at the top, watching the wheeling gulls and terns, or gazing down at the blue-green depths below.

One day Benjamin was doing just this, idly watching a man mooring his boat in a little creek immediately below him. Having moored the boat, the man stepped into a little dinghy he had pulled behind and, in doing so, dropped his wallet from his pocket. Down it went, zig-zagging through the clear water to lie on the sand on the seabed.

Unaware, he began to row ashore. Ben called, but in the splash of the oars, was unheard, so he scrambled down the rock, dived in and retrieved the wallet. He climbed into his own small dinghy and set off in pursuit. He later caught up to the man as he walked along the beach and who was not a little astonished to see a small, dripping wet boy holding out his wallet, having fancied himself entirely alone on the beach. He looked at Ben as if he thought he'd risen from the deep, as indeed he had!

We get many lovely pools left in the rocks around Herm when the tide goes out and we have got to know the ones where blennies live and the gobies with their bulgy, close together eyes. When the children were small they would crouch for hours over these pools, arms elbow deep in the water, trying to catch them. Blennies and gobies are nervous little fish, they are less than 6 inches long, but they are greedy and a few crumbs scattered in the water will often bring them out to investigate, whereupon a small brown hand would flash into action, and as often as not, emerge clutching a fish to be transferred to a waiting bucket. The occupation was never more than a trial of skill, and the end of the exercise always saw the bucket emptied back into the pool again to provide the quarry for the next occasion.

Later, as they grew older there would be more realistic fishing excursions. The lower rocks at the base of Caque Robert are a fine place for catching pollack and a strange long eel-like looking fish called long-nose or garfish, which have bright-blue bones and are good to eat when cut in inch-long slices and fried in butter.

Then there are sand eels, a sprat-like fish about 6 inches long, and at least once every summer when the tide is right we have a sand-eeling party. The eels are taken by night on a very low spring tide. Work for a sand-eeling party begins the day before when a huge bonfire of driftwood and pine logs is prepared on the dry sand at the top of Belvoir bay, well out of range of the tide. Alarm clocks are set for an hour before low water, usually about 1 a.m., and then we get off to bed good and early to snatch a few hours' sleep.

At the appointed time, warmly dressed against the cool night air, we arrive on the bay, armed with a frying pan, fat and loaves of bread. As the tide goes out the eels begin to leap from the sand, and, by the light of torches, we grab for them as they wriggle and flap at lightning speed across the wet sand. It is a dexterous business trying to keep a firm enough hold to fling them into a bucket before they wriggle free. On a good tide an astonishing number, many thousands, of eels appear and you can hear the slap and splash of them on all sides in the darkness.

Anyone approaching at such a time might be forgiven for thinking smugglers or wreckers were at work, as the beach is dotted with little lights moving quietly around.

When we have a bucket or two full, we retreat up the beach and light up the bonfire and, crouching round it, clean the fish, a simple enough operation involving only the removal of the head and gut. Then they are fried and sandwiched between two slices of dried bread and eaten. They are quite delicious.

Soon the pale-grey dawn creeps into the sky and Peter and I trudge home. The children wrap themselves in blankets by the fire and sleep the rest of the night away.

We have our fishing excursions during the winter months too, and then it is generally ormers we are after.

Ormers are a shellfish peculiar to the Channel Islands, although a somewhat larger variety is found in California and Australia where it is called an abalone. An ormer is a univalve which means that, unlike a scallop which is a bivalve, it has a shell on one side only and lives and grows clamped to the underside of rocks below tide level, so that they are only found on big spring tides, and one is only allowed to take them between October and May. The shells themselves are very beautiful, being ear shaped and lined with mother-of-pearl.

When we go ormering we put on rubber boots and plenty of warm clothes as it can be a cold job wading around in the icy water with your arms most of the time plunged to the elbows in the sea.

We turn over the rocks to search for the ormers, being careful afterwards to turn back the rocks so as not to disturb the marine growth that is the natural food of the ormers. Only medium-to large-sized ormers are taken and the small ones are left to mature and grow.

They say in Guernsey that more energy is expended on an ormer tide than at any other time of the year, and I'm sure it's true. Heaving over and then replacing huge boulders is no mean task. We always take with us on these excursions a bent skewer each with which to prise the ormer off the rock. When we have enough ormers in our bucket—say a couple of dozen or so—we take them home to prepare them for cooking. I have an understanding with my family that I will cook as many as they like but clean them I will not! It's quite a job. First they have to be cut out of their shells then scrubbed with a hard brush to remove the black slimy substance that adheres to them. Then they are beaten as you would a steak to make them tender. Some people declare that if left to soak in rain water for twelve hours this leaves them equally tender, but we prefer them beaten, with the taste of the sea water still in them.

Cooking is a comparatively simple matter as they are undoubtedly best just casseroled in a slow oven—their only accompaniment a bay leaf. They are quite delicious. Not particularly fishy in taste, they have their own unique flavour which is very hard to describe.

Prawns too are numerous around the coast. The best time for catching these is again on a big spring tide at low water. You wade ankle deep into the water, then stand still with your net held against the sea bed and facing towards the current, and then after standing still for a minute or two, when the water settles, you see the prawns swimming towards you. When one is over your net you raise it gently, so that it is unaware of any movement, and so lift it out of the water. It's generally—though by no means always—possible to get a good feed of prawns for two after about an hour's fishing.

Sometimes we are lucky enough to find a large flat fish lying in the sand at low water. I have actually stood on one before being aware of its presence, so still it is and so cleverly camouflaged, then there is a mad flurry of activity as it flaps wildly away, and we try to capture it—not always an easy thing to do.

122

Lurking in dark crevices among the rocks, we have found young octopus and squids, which flood the sea with an inky black fluid at the first approach of danger.

Searching for conger eel at low water is another popular pastime, not unspiced with the element of danger. They can be up to 5 or 6 feet long, and have huge jaws crammed with sharp teeth and a nasty habit of snapping viciously, so one goes armed with a stout, long-handled hook called a gaff, to prise them out of their holes. Congers are best eaten within hours of catching, so this is one fish which we never bring home from the market but cook only those we have caught ourselves. The head makes an excellent soup and the body, cut up into steaks and either baked or fried makes very good eating.

Where there is a conger eel there is not infrequently a lobster—the conger appears to play host and guardian to the lobster, so that having hooked out a conger from a deep rock crevice, a bit of further exploration with the gaff is often rewarded by finding a nice fat lobster. No one seems to understand why this association exists, but that it does is a fact.

Peter and the children were out ormering one day and each had with him a bent skewer and not the long-handled gaff with which they usually set forth, so that when Ben suddenly espied a lobster lurking in a long deep crevice they were ill-equipped to deal with it. The tide had turned and was rising rapidly so that there was no time to go back for a gaff. However, necessity being the mother of invention, they contrived a workable enough implement by tying a bent skewer to a particularly long and tough piece of seaweed of the type which we call 'lion's tail', using to bind it a grubby handkerchief which Rupert unearthed from his back pocket. The device worked well and they were rewarded for their ingenuity by hooking out a 3½-pounder, quite a fair size for a lobster.

Pennie

23

Mimosa

When Rosemary was 2, once again we set about alterations to the house—again to the kitchen. The children were growing, their legs were longer and we always seemed to be falling over each other in the combined cooking and dining area. This time we decided to take out the whole of the kitchen wall to the north and move forward in that direction to give ourselves a separate dining area. This constituted quite a large operation since the ground fell away on this side of the house and the kitchen was at second-storey level. Therefore there was a considerable amount of building up to be done from the ground.

Remembering what an uncomfortable time we had had when we had extended the living-room we decided that this time we would move out and away. Philip promised to oversee the work and see it through, so early in December we packed our bags and took ourselves off with all the children to Devonshire. We found a hotel high on Dartmoor and there we stayed for the next two months.

It was a happy, carefree time. I think we were ready for a holiday and we enjoyed it exceedingly. The wild wide rolling stretches of the moors seemed to us to be the perfect complement to our own pocket land, which we could compass in a morning's walk, and it was good to be able to stretch our legs—and our eyes—over such limitless terrain.

The moor was all around us and we did a lot of walking. The children had their first riding lessons on the shaggy Dartmoor ponies from a nearby stable.

In the New Year Peter and I arranged for a friend to come down to take care of the children and took ourselves up to London for a week. London was a bewildering but exciting change from both the island and the moors of Devonshire. Peter had one or two appointments which kept him busy and I spent most of my time wandering around the shops.

One morning I turned down Sloane Street, *en route* to a hair appointment, staring, as usual, into the shop windows as I went along. I was suddenly aware of being stared back at by a pair of button-round dark-brown eyes. They belonged to the most enchanting white and coffee-coloured Pekinese puppy who was sitting in a small basket alone in the window of a pet shop.

I can't really explain what happened next, but those brown eyes held a most compelling appeal and the next thing I knew I was inside the shop and the puppy was being lifted out of her basket and I was being covered with ecstatic warm, wet kisses. Ten minutes later I hurried out of the shop and to the hairdresser's. Back in the pet shop the Pekinese was having her pedigree forms filled in and arrangements were being made to give her her injections. I was to collect her just before midday.

I sat under the drier in a daze. What had I done? What on earth would Peter say? We hadn't discussed having another dog, still less a small Pekinese. I had an uneasy feeling that Peter really only liked large dogs. I gazed round, slightly distraught. The wallpaper in the salon was pale grey with sprigs of golden mimosa springing across it. Well, there was a name for her at any rate! Mimosa. It would suit her well with her light golden patches and ears. Just before midday I was back at the shop. She looked beautiful, she had just been shampooed and had a brush and comb and I picked up the soft, quivering little thing and walked outside the shop just in time to see Peter coming round the corner on his way back to our hotel.

He saw me and crossed the street. I stood transfixed.

"Hello," he said. "What an adorable puppy!" He fondled her ears and I breathed more easily. He stood caressing the dog for a minute or two, then, "Well, you'd better take it back into the shop now—we must hurry along. I've got another appointment immediately after lunch."

I drew a deep breath. "I can't take her back—you see, I've just bought her."

Peter stared at me unbelievingly. It was the first time that either of us had behaved in such a unilateral way and taken a major decision without consulting the other. I stared back and, after a moment's silence, Peter turned on his heel and walked away and into the hotel.

I turned and looked back at the pet shop. It had turned twelve and the door was shut and the window lights were out. It was empty. Moreover, it was a Saturday and wouldn't be open again until Monday. I followed Peter back to the hotel and told him that I would take the puppy back to the shop on Monday. He gave a non-committal grunt and retired behind his newspaper.

Well, anyway, I should have to look after her for the weekend. I fitted out the bathroom with newspaper and made her up a bed in a cardboard box. Mimosa must have known what was in the wind, because if ever a dog set about ingratiating herself into our favour, she did. She was clean and obviously house-trained—which, in such a young puppy, impressed us both. She produced every endearing trick she knew and persisted in making much of Peter, whose resistance crumbled in no time at all.

Monday came and not a word was said about returning her. Tuesday saw us carefully packing her cardboard box on to the back seat of the car and a gaily smiling Pekinese puppy setting forth for Devonshire.

No need to wonder how the children would react. Their delight in the newest and youngest member of the family knew no bounds. We don't like to think now of how we nearly didn't keep Mimosa, but we often talk of the extraordinary odds that operated to remove her from a life of walking in the parks and on the pavements of London to the carefree unrestricted life she enjoys today in a little island 20 miles from the French coast, where she is free to run at will and explore exciting country smells with each shining hair of her coat alive with enjoyment.

Her little body stays slim and fit and she is ever ready to accompany us wherever we may walk about the island. Never, however, has she developed a love of the sea, and she has made it quite clear from the start that she is no sea dog. Boats are not for her and no sooner is she in one than she begins an uncontrollable shivering and beads of perspiration break out across her upper lip. Neither will she swim or paddle. She follows us on to the beach and loves the sand, but will pick her way delicately along the edge of the sea with a wary eye on any wave that might break over her feet.

Back on the island again after our winter sojourn on Dartmoor, we settled comfortably into our much-improved house. Shortly after our return we learnt that work was being done on the airport in Guernsey, which involved the use of some heavy excavating equipment. Work was held up due to the weather and the machinery stood idle. Peter seized the opportunity to borrow one of the large mechanical diggers—a Drott—to perform some much needed excavating work in Herm.

The Drott was floated across on a huge flat barge, pulled by two launches, and we were all down to watch it arrive, surely the largest cargo ever to be landed on the island.

The chief task we wanted done was the establishment of a path right round the island. Apart from the drive climbing to the top of the hill from the harbour and the central spine road running from north to south, the island was served by small, ill-made paths which were little more than rabbit tracks. Quite apart from our own convenience, now that so many

127

more people were visiting the island it was highly desirable to open up more of the land and make it accessible. The coastline of Herm is heavenly and we thought how lovely it would be to be able to walk right round it without scrambling and struggling as was the case.

The Drott set to work and I was immediately appalled by the ugly scars that began to wind itself round the island.

"In a couple of months time you'll not see these piles of earth on either side of the track," Peter assured me, but even he was unprepared for what in fact happened.

By May thousands and thousands of foxgloves had sprung up in the newly turned earth on either side, forming a purple rampart of bloom against the azure sea. We had never seen anything so magnificent. We wondered whether the seeds had lain dormant in the earth through countless centuries since the land was last turned over, or was it that the foxgloves seed is always widely and thickly dispersed in Herm, and that they took advantage of this virgin soil and prospered so? They still appear on either side of this coastal track, but not in the same profusion as they did that first time.

When Ben was approaching his eighth birthday we asked him what he would like for his birthday. Somewhat diffidently he replied, "Well, there's something I'd like very much indeed, but I don't know whether you'll give it to me or not."

Expecting to hear it was a speedboat or something equally impossible to grant we nevertheless asked him what it was.

"Tom Cat," he replied. Tom was of quite ordinary farm origins and we had already had him in the house for about four years. The rest of the family were persuaded to agree to this transfer of ownership, so very solemnly the birthday presentation was made, and instead of being a family cat Tom became Ben's.

He has grown into the most enormous cat, which isn't surprising as he's a prodigious rabbiter and must account for at least a couple of rabbits a day. Birds, I'm glad to say, he leaves severely alone, as Peter gave him a serious talking to about it when he was young. He has a predilection for camping and spends a large part of the summer in Little Seagull with various families who happen to be camping there. He had, however, to be dissuaded from his tendency to live not 'under canvas' but 'over canvas' and more than one startled camper has awakened in the night to the sudden screech of Tom's claws as he glissaded down the roof of the tent from the top to bottom, so Peter had to speak to him about that too. By a happy coincidence he is an almost exact match to Mimosa, golden-brown and white. He has a special affinity for Ben and on more than one occasion when Ben has been arriving home on the island for his school holidays he seems to sense his return and will be found waiting on the end of the harbour for him—a place he is never normally to be seen.

24

History—Old and New

Ever since we had been living on the island we had been avid for any information we could glean about the early history of Herm. This we found most difficult to collect together, as much of it has passed unrecorded, and we have spent many hours in the Guille Alles Library in Saint Peter Port, poring over documents and books, and come away little the wiser. But thanks to the help of a friend living in Guernsey, who has spent even longer unravelling Herm's history, we have learnt a certain amount.

The history of the little church interested us especially and it seems to be a story of frequent change. It appears that Christianity was first brought to the Channel Islands as early as the fourth or fifth century. In A.D. 565 Saint Magloire travelling from Brittany established monasteries in Jersey and Sark, and it is doubtless from the latter island that monks first set foot on Herm. It is fascinating to picture them setting forth in their sailing boats to explore both Herm and Jethou. They built a little chapel on a reef between these two islands, which was at that time dry land, as the sea level was about thirty feet lower than it is today, and they dedicated it to Saint Magloire, whose origins before he went to Brittany were probably Irish. Local folklore has it that a great storm divided Herm from Jethou, in A.D. 709. Whether this is true or not is hard to say, but it is certain that sea now covers the place where once the chapel stood, and nothing now remains, although it is said that it was still visible under the sea as late as the middle of the last century.

The little chapel that stands at the top of the hill was probably built during the time of Robert, Duke of Normandy, in about A.D. 1050. He gave Herm to the Benedictine Abbey of Mont Saint Michel, and monks of this order remained on the island for about thirty years. Later the island was given to an Augustinian order by William the Conqueror, and these monks remained many years.

They farmed the island extensively, and many of the huge granite walls surrounding the gardens and the dry-stone walls dividing the fields no doubt date from this time. The extensiveness of these never fail to astonish us, and the number of man hours which went into their construction must have been truly astronomical. The pioneering spirit of the monks must have made possible a task which would daunt many a present-day landowner.

It was not until some centuries later, in 1480, that there is first mention of Saint Tugual—the name by which the chapel is known today. It is thought that he accompanied Saint Magloire to Herm in the first place, nine hundred years earlier, and that is why the church was re-dedicated to him sometime after Saint Magloire's death.

People sometimes ask me what denomination the church is and this being difficult to answer I say, "Non-denominational." But whatever it is, this I know, it has great charm and peacefulness. Quite small, the nave is only about 30 feet long, and the only transept, which faces northwards, is 17 feet; the church has sturdy granite walls all of 2 feet thick and the stone-arched roof is of the same thickness. The monks built this arched roof in a strangely simple manner. The church walls were built up to the point from which the arch was to spring and then the whole of the building was hard packed with earth. The earth was then carried on as one might build a sandcastle into the shape of the roof, after which the stones for the roof were laid in place on the earth right up to the keystones at the top. When all the stones were in place the earth was then removed.

When we first came to Herm the church was virtually unfurnished; there were only some rickety old chairs and a little brass cross on the altar. We soon began to acquire the necessary furnishings, firstly by buying forty new light-oak chairs. A guest in the hotel gave us three specially made forms which matched the chairs and which we put in the north transept to be used by the children. These chairs and forms together seat as many as the church will hold. We bought a very old American organ for £10, and a very good 'buy' it was. It is as good today as it was then, and in the hands of a competent organist, and assisted by the remarkable acoustic properties of the church, it produces a very fine noise indeed. A woman in Guernsey gave us a wooden crucifix which her brother had picked up and put in his knapsack as he crawled through a ruined church under gunfire in France during the 1914-18 war. The metal figure of Christ has several dents where a piece of shrapnel hit it.

Recently Peter fitted a miniature carved oak ship's figurehead in the form of an angel—a relic of the great ship-building days in Guernsey—to the underside of the lectern. The altar cloth is an old, heavy Victorian bedsheet, with the initials S.E.W., embroidered on it—Peter's grandparents'.

There has always been a very old, high-backed wooden chair with arms in the church and we put this on one side of the altar dais. We call it 'the Bishop's chair' now because when the Bishop of Winchester comes to stay with us, which he does from time to time, he always asks if he "may help with the service", and when he does so he sits in his chair, clad in all his robes and with his crook, a genuine shepherd's crook just like the ones used by the shepherds of Hampshire, at his side.

The church itself was in good structural condition. It has stood for nearly one thousand years and is good for many more, but the pleasing simplicity of its lines was lost at the west end in the welter of undergrowth which crept right up to the west door—so much so, in fact, that we could hardly use that door at all. It had to remain like that for many years until in the order of priority we could get around to doing something about it, and it must have been about 1960 before that time arrived.

We got Paul to pull down the ramshackle old greenhouse that leant drunkenly against the high northern wall of the manor garden where it abutted on the church, and to clear back the tangle of bramble and briar and vine that choked that corner, hiding the lovely little belfry from view, and thus discovered for the first time what an attractive, sheltered corner of the garden this could become.

Over the years we had got to know a Scotsman, Jimmie, who was a mason. He lived in Guernsey and came across from time to time and stayed in one of the cottages when we had any walling to do which we wanted to be especially well made. He was a real craftsman and worked with speed and deftness, and his walls were full of texture and life. I had never realised before I met Jimmie how much artistry could go into the making of a wall.

We called Jimmie over now and discussed with him the making of a little walled garden outside the west door of the church. He built us a low stone wall across one end of the larger garden to enclose a rectangle of lawn in one corner of which stood the belfry tower, and then constructed a small terrace outside the west door so that one entered the garden from the church down two steps. We intended to pave the terrace with old bricks laid in a herring-bone pattern as soon as we could find some suitable bricks.

The children took a great interest in the making of this garden, and, as Jimmie was a firm favourite with them all, there was usually one or other of them to be found helping him. Pulling the ivy away from the church wall one day they discovered an old iron pump with the date 1867 inscribed on the front. They found it was still in working order and, at Mrs. Corboy's suggestion, they begged a tin of green paint and carefully painted it.

One day when the wall was nearly completed they handed Jimmie a sealed jar containing a paper on which was written the date and all their names and ages and asked him to build it into the wall so that one day, generations hence, perhaps someone might find it and know the names of all the children

133

at that time and how they had helped to make the garden. We planted honeysuckle up the high sheltering north wall together with climbing roses and these have grown so that now they completely cover it and on a sunny summer's day fill the garden with their fragrance.

Around the other sides of the small lawn we planted lavender and roses and many bulbs and it was amazing how, almost from the first, the little garden acquired an atmosphere so that after the service on Sundays people linger there and seem loth to leave its sequestered calm.

We have always had a family service there on Sunday from the first autumn in 1949 when Jo was christened. Taken by Peter it is short and simple and the island children have always taken a large part in it, even when they were quite small, from ringing the bell—frequently Rupert's job— to playing the organ—which first Jo, and later Penny, learnt to do. Two children usually read the lessons—the very small ones reading from a child's stories of Jesus.

One summer the Vicar of Battersea visited us and in the course of conversation said that in his parish in Battersea he had a boys' club which was sponsored by Caius College, Cambridge. I told him that that had been my brother Geoffrey's college. Later when we showed him the little chapel he looked at the well-worn altar frontal and said that he would send us one that he had, one that had been salvaged from a bombed-out church in Battersea. It arrived a few days after his return to London with a note to say would we please accept it in memory of Geoffrey and remembering all that Caius College had done for his boys' club. It is a lovely thing of figured ivory silk with two lilies embroidered in blue and gold on either side of a central golden cross.

Besides the garden we have made one other addition to the church and this is a window high in the south-facing wall of the church near the altar.

Dad had always loved the little church and attended our services there whenever he was on the island, and one day he asked us if he could give us a stained-glass window for it. We accepted his offer with delight and together we decided on its site and design. He commissioned a firm of stained-glass makers in Exeter to do it and some months later, when we visited him in his home at Torquay, he showed us the final drawings they had sent him. We were thrilled. We had chosen for the theme Christ stilling the waters from the bows of the boat on Gallilee and the picture he showed us was more impressive than we had dared to hope it could be.

Christ was depicted standing up in the bows, His stern calm face in sharp contrast to the anxious expressions on the faces of the disciples crouched at His feet and gazing up at Him. Waves lashed at the sides of the boat. The colours of the robes and the sea and sky were vivid and rich and glowing.

Dad was pleased with our enthusiasm for it and instructed the work on the window to be put in hand. The window has a special significance now for Peter and me because that was the last time we saw Dad alive. He died a few weeks afterwards and before the window he had given us was completed.

When it was at last in place in the church we had a service of commemoration and dedication on a bright sunny day in August and the sun streamed through the window and threw bright colours across the front of the altar cloth.

25

Our Ghostly Resident

After we had been living in Herm for some few years we became aware that we shared the island with a ghost. The stories were varied and from a number of different sources, but all told of a monk clad in a dark brown habit and, strange to say, everyone who claimed to have seen him had been not the least bit scared or worried. He was obviously a very friendly ghost and shed a positively benign influence.

There was Pat's story how, living in one of the farm cottages, she had awoken one night and seen a figure wearing a monk's habit sitting on a low stool by the window gazing out to sea. His back was towards her and she couldn't see his face. She turned to rouse her husband and when she looked back again the monk was no longer there.

There was another girl who was walking through the arched passageway by the keep one night when she saw what she took to be her husband in his duffle coat turn the corner in front of her. She ran to catch him up but when she rounded the corner herself there was no one there.

And there was the farm foreman who entered the chapel late one night to see if the windows were secure against the rising wind and who saw a monk kneeling in front of the altar who suddenly wasn't there any more.

Strangest of all was the clairoyant's story. She was staying as a guest in the hotel and one day she approached Peter and asked him:

"Will the monk be taking the service in the chapel on Sunday?"

"The monk—who do you mean?" replied Peter, mystified.

"I've just been speaking to him on the lawn outside the hotel—he's a very charming gentleman," she answered.

"But we have no monks on the island." Peter told her. The woman was not at all nonplussed and immediately averred that her companion had evidently been of the spirit world and told Peter that if she were fortunate enough to meet him again she would learn more about him. Peter sceptically agreed that this would be a good idea.

A few days later she was able to tell him that the monk's name was Pierre du Pont and that he had lived on the island in the eleventh century and she thought that there had been a massacre on the island and that he had been burnt at the stake.

Peter and I cannot claim to have seen him at all, although I had one strange experience down in the hotel one evening.

I was playing cards with three friends and Sapper was stretched out on the rug at our feet in front of the fire. All at once he lifted his head, got to his feet and with slowly rising hackles gazed at the door. Gradually his head turned and his eyes followed the progress of someone, or something, right across the room towards the door on the opposite side. Not a thing was visible to the three of us watching. Rather an eerie experience.

Another peculiar incident happened one autumn. We had been taking some photographs up in our walled garden. When the film was developed, in the centre of one of the photographs showing the long sloping stretch of lawn running down to the garden wall appeared a large bonfire where none had been and in the centre of the flames the vague but easily descernible outlines of a face. We have shown this photograph to a number of people, and it is only fair to say that at least half of them put it down to a photographic error in the developing process.

There is no particular place on the island associated with his appearance, indeed, as yet no two people claim to have seen him in the same place, but the stories keep recurring fairly persistently.

137

There does seem to be some historical basis for the presence of the ghost. We know that monks inhabited the island, and there is moreover, a strong local legend to support the story of the massacre. We know that in 1541 there was a rising clash of conflicting creeds in the Channel Islands, with Roman Catholics fast becoming outnumbered by Calvinists and Protestants. The local legend relates that: "All the Roman Catholics in the other islands fled to Herm, and there attempted to hold out against the Protestant onslaught. But superior numbers prevailed, the besieged were starving, and were forced to capitulate. The honourable terms agreed upon by the victors were repudiated, and most of the monks, together with 400 refugees were slaughtered."

For my part, if Pierre du Pont is at all responsible for the tranquil, benign atmosphere on the island, I hope he will stay with us for a long time.

There is only one place on Herm which I find strangely disquieting. On the lower slopes of Petit Monceau and Grande Monceau, twin hills which form the southern boundary of the common, are several Neolithic graves— in fact the whole of the northern part of the island was used as a burial ground some three or four thousand years ago.

There has been evidence of so many burials there, that they cannot possibly all have been of a resident Herm population, and there is no doubt that Herm was used as a burial ground, not only for people living in Guernsey, but also from the neighbouring coast of Normandy, as it is thought that those Neolithic people believed that the spirits of the departed could not cross water, and so would be unable to return to haunt them.

Under the shelter of the two hills one can still discern in the configuration of the ground a vast amphitheatre where ancient burial rites no doubt took place. Although I love most of the common this particular place has to me a strange haunted air as if great emotions have been roused here at some time, and which still linger to charge the atmosphere with their presence.

26

Boats

Boats and the weather have a tendency to dominate our lives living in Herm, and a day is gauged, not so much by whether the sun shines as to what the sea is like, and what the problems of communication are likely to be. If the sea is rough it is not only a question of whether the boat will come across or not, but when will be the best time. An ebb tide and a strong south wind is a bad combination and so the boat must wait to come across until the tide is flowing and high enough to enable it to get into the harbour, where, on arrival, it will be more protected from the wind than at Rosiere Steps, and where the unloading of stores is easier. These decisions we leave to the skipper of the boat, and abide absolutely by what he decides.

I remember with mortification how during our very early days the then skipper of the boat was discussing with Peter as to whether the boat should make the trip or not. It was a rough, unpleasant day and, although I had made no plans to go over, Peter hoped to do so and I felt anxious and said so. Peter turned to me and said, "All right then, you make the decision. Does the boat go or doesn't it?"

"No," I replied, "it doesn't, it's too rough."

The skipper gave a bad-tempered growl, turned on his heel and stumped off muttering, "Damned if I'll stand for petticoat rule," and that same day handed in his notice. He was with difficulty persuaded to withdraw it, and I had learnt my lesson.

We have had three different boats since we came to Herm. First there was the *Celia*, a 20-ton part-decked cargo launch, who finished her useful seagoing life in about 1950. After the *Celia* came the *Arrowhead*, a 42-foot ex-Admiralty harbour launch. The children felt nostalgic when the *Henry Rose II* came to supersede the *Arrowhead*, for they had known her all their lives and she had indeed performed Trojan service for us, battling through great seas in the winter in the able hands of Len, her skipper, and keeping the island supplied with day-to-day shipment of stores. But travelling in the *Arrowhead* could be pretty rugged and many times have we made the crossing on a cold rough day huddled beneath dripping tarpaulins with huge waves seemingly about to surge into the boat itself. Moreover she had given us some anxious moments in the past. Chief among these I remember one particular incident.

Sir William Penney, at that time Britain's leading atomic scientist, along with some senior members of the States of Guernsey, had been visiting the island. It was low tide when they came to leave and Peter and I saw them off from Rosaire Steps. When the boat was about a quarter of a mile out to sea we were surprised to see that it had stopped. Bearing, as it did, such illustrious company, Peter was concerned that the return trip was not running to schedule, but when later he learnt the reason for the delay, he was horrified. The pipe leading to the petrol engine had fractured and the boat had stopped to make temporary repairs. She had then limped back to Guernsey with the bilges awash with petrol. It would only have needed a spark from someone's cigarette falling into the bottom of the boat to have ensured the most hideous of catastrophes. As

140

soon as it was feasible we replaced the petrol engine with a diesel one—a considerably safer proposition.

The *Henry Rose II* is a bigger boat and possesses besides a diesel engine, a ship's radio and directional finding equipment. She rides considerably higher out of the water and two-thirds of her deck space is covered in, so, even under bad winter conditions, the crossing can be made in a measure of comfort, and safety too—both important ingredients to all of us.

Boating in the winter with all its aspects of braving the elements, and when we have to rely entirely on our boat, is a very different thing to making the trip to Guernsey during the summer months. Then there is a fleet of boats plying from Guernsey to choose from, and almost every year a new and splendid craft makes its appearance on the water, including two smart speedboats, which skim across like twin arrows, and make the trip in just about eight minutes. Then for the most part, boating is pleasurable and I never step into the boat without thinking, if I lived in England I should be getting into a car now, or a train or a bus. How much nicer this is!

It was a fact that the longer I stayed in Herm without going across the 3 miles to Guernsey the less I wanted to go, and the more difficult I found it to contemplate a day spent in the busy thrust of a town. Noticing this Peter said I was in danger of becoming a cabbage or even neurotic about it. I didn't think that exactly but nevertheless, on the principle that 'he knows not Herm who only Herm knows', I agreed with him that I ought to make the effort to go across to Guernsey more frequently. In fact, once I had summoned up the necessary determination, I always enjoyed a day in Saint Peter Port.

Arriving by sea, Saint Peter Port has a most attractive appearance. It clusters round the harbour and up the hill behind, its high narrow buildings and steeply sloping roofs looking much more Breton French than English, and when one considers its history and its geographical position this is hardly surprising, even though English is the tongue one hears on every hand. Regrettably the old Guernsey patois is seldom heard. Even so, there is a lilt and inflexion to the speech of a

141

Guernseyman that gives the impression that one is listening to another language.

Many of the streets have old French names and are cobbled and steep, and many are not streets at all but are steep flights of steps leading from one level of the town to another.

The most fascinating aspects of the town are the markets. They are in a high vaulted building with three different halls. The fish market is alive, literally, with shell fish of every description and many other locally caught fish, including octopus and conger eels, flat fish regarding one with glassy stare and, if the season is right, box after box of shining, curled, beautifully marked blue-green mackerel. Then there is the flower and fruit market where each stall vies with the next in a riot of colour and perfume; glowing grapes cascade from the stalls piled high with shining tomatoes, purple aubergines and scarlet and green peppers, and golden melons. The third hall is the meat market, where the floor is strewn with sawdust and the open-fronted booths are hung with poultry and sides of beef, pork and veal.

Once we visited the market on Christmas Eve. Holly and ivy festooned the booths and through the halls walked the church choir in their scarlet and white robes and carrying lanterns as they sang Christmas hymns and carols. Round them bobbed a group of children, eyes sparkling and cheeks rosy with excitement. The whole scene was pure Dickens in character.

Then after a day in Guernsey there is the boat trip back again, usually as enjoyable and restful as the outward morning one. But one return trip sticks in my mind. It was during the first winter after we came to Herm. We had sailed across in the morning under near perfect conditions, but during the day the weather worsened and by evening a stiff wind blew. It was just before Christmas and almost all the island inhabitants were on board, laden with Christmas parcels.

We had arranged with the boatman to sail promptly at 4 p.m., but when we arrived at the quay to embark it was to find that he had negligently allowed the boat to dry out on the falling tide and it would not float again until 5.30 p.m., by which time it would be already dark. Such were our family arrangements that we had almost no option but to make the return trip, although I think that if Peter and Philip had realised just what was in store for us they would have called it off, and those left on Herm, children and all, would just have had to manage as best they could. When we did embark it was to find the boat piled high with baled hay which covered the life rafts. We perched ourselves and our packages on top of them, under the canvas awning. The wind was south-westerly so that it was not until we had passed out through the harbour mouth that its true strength was felt, and by this time it was gale force. Suddenly in pitch darkness and with no leading lights ahead the boat dropped into the trough of a wave which, towering above us, rushed towards us. Violently the *Celia* responded, only to surge down into the next trough, and by now we were surrounded by a welter of vicious, thundering sea, breaking white all around us in the darkness.

We had no great confidence in our boatman of those days—the dependable old man who we had inherited with the island had retired, and we were served as an interim measure while we searched for a reliable skipper by a shiftless individual with a regrettable predilection for the bottle. On this occasion he had undoubtedly spent most of his afternoon ashore in one of the quayside pubs.

We ploughed on into the darkness, and it was a fact that once we had cleared the pier heads it was safer to continue ahead than to attempt to turn round and put ourselves broadside on to the mountainous waves.

We have electric leading lights on Herm now, but at that time there was not so much as a glimmer of light to be seen on the island. With most of us, myself included, it was fortunately a case of where ignorance is bliss, but Peter and Philip were acutely conscious of the danger. They were desperately worried and blamed themselves for ever allowing the boat to put to sea so late in the darkness and without realising the state of the skipper. They positioned themselves either side of him and did what they could to sober him up and keep his mind on the job of bringing us safely to port.

We did eventually make our little harbour, and Peter, helping us ashore, determined that in future any return shopping trip should be accomplished in daylight. This has been so ever since.

The boatman was summarily dismissed and, fortunately, very soon replaced.

Mostly, however, the return trip is uneventful and our chief concern is that the tide should be high enough to allow the boat to get into the harbour and so save the labour of climbing up the steep steps of Rosaire and the walk back along the winding lane to the village.

Once back in Herm the peace and quiet laps round us again, and the busy little town seems much, much farther away than just 3 miles across the water.

puttin   Pennie

27

Birds of Herm

Ever since Peter Scott, and later Kay, kindled our interest in the birds of Herm, we have become continually more aware of them and we often think how fortunate we are to have not only sea birds, but also a great variety of land-birds who either nest here or visit us on their migratory routes. The island is an almost complete 'bird world' in miniature, and over the years we have seen most British species.

Looking through Kay's bird book I see that she has ticked and marked a date against 107 different species all seen during one year.

To the visitor, of course, the sea birds are the most noticeable. They wake to the call of the gulls and the shrill piping of the oyster-catchers.

There are three nesting varieties of gulls here, the herring and lesser black-backed gulls being the most common, and there are a few of the huge and voracious greater black-backed variety. Majestic though these are in flight, they nevertheless have some cruel and unpleasant habits. We have stood on the cliffs at the south end of the island and seen a greater black-backed gull lying in wait for a puffin as it emerged from its burrow, pick it up by the scruff of its neck and then fly off with it out to sea, whereupon the gull holds its head under the water to drown it before flying off to devour it.

The puffins nest in a small colony on top of one of the cliffs facing Sark. The cliff top is honeycombed with their burrows, some of which they have taken over from their former tenants, the rabbits. We are always astonished to watch them arriving to feed their young with anything up to seven or eight sand-eels hanging crosswise from their enormous multi-coloured beaks. How on earth do they catch so many on one excursion without letting the first ones go?

We have a great number of cormorants and shags. It is extremely difficult to tell the difference between them, except at very close range, and we are inclined to think that the majority of these rather ugly, long-necked black birds are shags. Sitting in Belvoir bay any summer morning, you can see them flying in line ahead just above the water across the bay from the south, north to their feeding ground up beyond the Shell Beach, and then in the evening, see them returning, still in line. Sometimes we see them fishing as they go, and realise that there must be a shoal of mackerel beneath them. They have an amusing leap-frog action. The leader will suddenly dive, whilst a new bird proceeds to lead the line, the old leader suddenly popping up at the back, and then down goes the new leader and another takes over and so on. It's a fascinating sight to watch.

The tern, or sea swallow, is a frequent sight in Belvoir bay, and there are colonies nesting on the outlying islets, although they occasionally nest on our north beach. They are surely the most graceful of all sea birds, looking like ballet dancers pirouetting over the wave tops. In great contrast to their light and airy flight and dive is the swift, sure plummeting of the gannet, which we frequently watch fishing all around our shores. They are huge white birds, with black-tipped wings

146

which span up to 6 feet, and to see them hurtling out of the sky, with closed wings, to disappear in a little fountain of spray is a sight not to be forgotten. There is a colony of these birds nesting on a rocky stack off the north-west corner of Alderney. Once, on a childhood holiday in Scotland, an old fisherman told me that the inhabitants of Saint Kilda far out in the Atlantic used to kill the gannets for food, by the simple expedient of floating a green board on the sea with a fish nailed to it. The unfortunate birds diving for the fish broke their necks on the board. Rather a horrid story and not one that I have heard hereabouts.

In contrast to the birds of the cliffs at the south end of the island, walking round the sand dunes of the north end you can see many of the smaller breeds of sea birds which frequent the shore and water's edge. The turnstones, scurrying around like large chestnut-coloured mice; dunlin; sandpipers and sanderling, all busily exploring the sea-shore for fish remains, worms, sandhoppers and other insects.

Amongst the more numerous land birds we have are linnets, meadow pippets, wheatears, many varieties of warblers and, strangely, cuckoos, who for so small an island are always in great evidence in the spring.

In August flocks of goldfinch frequent the thistle beds around the island, and they are very easy to pick out, with their distinctive gold and black barred wings and red faces.

We have an enormous number of wrens, and one ornithologist who frequently stays here says that he has never known such a density of wrens over a comparable area. He thinks it possible also that the Herm wrens have certain indigenous peculiarities, and he doubts if they ever leave the island. *British Birds* already recognise the existence of three separate island breeds, Saint Kilda, Shetland and Hebridean. Could it be that there is also a Herm variety? Certain it is that our wrens appear to have very much brighter and stronger markings than those I see in my native Yorkshire.

Apart from our resident birds, we have a number of interesting visitors, of these the hoopoe is perhaps the most strange. He looks like some rare exotic bird which has escaped

147

from an aviary, with his fantastic fan-shaped, cinnamon-coloured crest and long curved bill. We see him here and there about the island for a few days, and then he goes on his way. Another colourful visitor is the kingfisher, who, astonishing as it may sound, visits us from time to time, and appears to take up temporary quarters in the harbour wall. He doesn't come every year but we are always glad when someone reports having seen a flash of sapphire-blue dart across the harbour and we realise that the kingfisher has come to spend a few days with us again.

We have seen a flock of twenty heron wading around among the off-shore islets, a group of four owls flying about the rocky scars bordering the common, and once we saw a spoonbill.

One night recently a little brown bird flew into the house and, bemused by the light, fluttered frantically around. Jo caught it and, remarking the russet-coloured tail and whitish-brown breast, we were able to identify it as a nightingale.

Sometimes we get birds resting with us that have been blown off course and arrive in an exhausted condition. I remember picking up a snow bunting once down by Fisherman's Cottage. He stayed resting for almost a week before being strong enough to fly on. In the summer of 1971 we had a grey-lag goose with us, for over a week. He appeared one evening off the harbour, obviously hungry and tired. We fed him and he became quite friendly and would come quite close inshore when we were swimming.

I think the bird that astonished us most was an elegant rosy-pink bird with remarkably long neck and legs, that we saw one day, picking its way among the boulders on the beach by the harbour. The wing quills were black and the bill bent abruptly downwards. It was clearly none other than a flamingo. We contacted the zoo in Guernsey but they disclaimed any knowledge of a flamingo being at large and the mystery as to where it came from remained unsolved. The only thing we can think of is that some person in Guernsey keeps flamingoes in their garden and it had flown over to us, but we have not heard of this being the case.

28

A very Memorable Occasion

One might suppose that living in Herm, the circle of people one met would inevitably be very prescribed, but this has proved to be anything but the case. Visiting us as a day's respite from commitments in Guernsey have been Cabinet Ministers, film stars, pop artists and a wide range of civic and public dignitaries. On one occasion we were asked to arrange lunch for an official party which included a Cabinet Minister and other members of the British government who were in Guernsey on matters of state. Thinking that after a round of official functions they might well appreciate some-thing more informal, we decided to give them a picnic lunch. The boat landed at Rosiere and Peter, meeting them there, led them by the narrow winding cliff path to where the tractor waited. They were all very much in 'city suiting' and the sight of black bowler hats bobbing through the bracken was an incongruous one indeed. We had equipped the tractor trailer with bales of straw as improvised seating, and a very fine charabanc it made as Peter drove them on a conducted tour of the island, finishing up at a heavenly site we had prepared, right on the south end of the island. The picnic was a great success. It was a warm sunny day, and as lunch proceeded, first one jacket was removed, and then another, followed by ties, and shirt sleeves were rolled up. Sitting there in the sunshine, with Sark and Jersey lying to the south and the French coast clearly visible to the east across a stretch of shimmering sea, it must have seemed a far cry from the noise and bustle of Westminster.

149

Most popular among the younger members of the island community have been the visits of Cliff Richard. Indeed all of us have fallen under the spell of his charm and friendliness. He has come from time to time and spent a week or two under canvas, camping with a troop of 'Crusaders' as one of their officers, and we have joined with them in their camp fire barbeques and, led by Cliff, sung songs far into the night. He has joined the little service in the church on Sundays, and the songs he sang there to his guitar must surely have added a page to its one thousand years of history. Certainly his rendering of "When I Survey The Wondrous Cross" is as moving and reverent as anything those old walls can ever have absorbed.

But for Peter and me, undoubtedly the greatest thrill came in the summer of 1957. The Queen and the Duke of Edinburgh were to visit Guernsey in the *Britannia*, which was to lie off the island outside Saint Peter Port harbour. We were all very excited as we would have a grandstand view from Herm, and then a few weeks before the visit Peter and I received an invitation to an evening reception on board the *Britannia*. We were thrilled beyond measure and looked forward to the day with eager anticipation.

The evening before 26th July was still and clear and everything seemed to be set fair for the morrow. I woke up next morning to hear a dismayed, "Oh *No!*" from Peter. A thick rainy mist shrouded the island and blew damply in from the sea with a fresh to strong wind behind it. The foghorn moaned dismally and we could hardly see the end of the garden.

The royal yacht was due to arrive off Guernsey at 10.30 a.m., but under these weather conditions would she come? We spent an anxious morning, the mist continued to shroud everything thickly and the wind blew strongly from the south-west.

At midday Peter and I walked to the look-out, the low escarpment overlooking the sea near the farm buildings. We peered into the mist and then suddenly, as we watched, a shaft of sunlight pierced the fog. Within seconds a patch of

150

blue sky appeared and, like the curtains of a stage, the mist curled swiftly back. Within minutes the scene was transformed, the sea which such a short time before had appeared grey and cold was now a dazzling blue, flecked with little white-capped waves and dancing with sparkles of light; and there, unbelievably handsome, lay the *Britannia*. Our hearts lifted at the sight and we were immensely relieved, though our relief was somewhat tempered by anxiety, for the wind was still fresh and might strengthen further, in which case the reception might be cancelled and, in any case, we might have difficulty getting away from the island to attend it.

In size the *Britannia* looked as it lay there to be half as big again as the mail steamers which ply between England and the islands, but so flawless in design that elegance, not size, was the thing that impressed us about her.

The wind moved up a point or two to the north and the sky became bluer and brighter and soon the sun shone from a cloudless sky. The wind remained fresh but not unduly so, and six o'clock that evening saw us setting off down the hill resplendent in evening dress, and stepping on board the *Arrowhead en route* for the royal yacht.

It was a memorable and wonderful evening. We were presented to Her Majesty and also had a conversation with Prince Philip.

I remember how, as I curtseyed to the Queen, I was thinking, "This is a moment you will be able to recapture all your life," and I know I always will. It was an immensely proud moment.

The Queen asked me about life on the island, how many families there were, and about the island school, whilst Prince Philip questioned Peter about the practical difficulties and economic problems of running the island, and compared it to an island he knew on Lake Constance.

When the reception was over and the Queen and the Duke had left, there was a movement among the guests to leave. Peter and I were in no hurry. We stood patiently to one side admiring the beautiful reception room where we stood; it had

151

all the elegance and comfort of a London drawing-room whilst yet retaining an indefinable ship-board quality.

Eventually we went ashore in the last launch load—it turned out to be the royal barge itself which took us, the one used by H.M. the Queen herself, a lovely craft with white leather upholstery and shining brass fittings.

Next day the *Britannia* sailed for Jersey. We all gathered on the south point of the island to watch her pass by and we waved flags and cheered.

The family in the Arrowhead.

The daffodil harvest (*right*). The lighter side of schooldays: the conjurer entertains *en route* to Herm.

The farm cottages in 1950, prior to starting work on them; and as they are today.

Peter, Mimosa and
I enjoy a quiet day
at Belvoir.

(Right) Peter and me in St Tugal's chapel as we first found it, unfurnished and unused; and below as it is today.

29

Woolly Bear

When Jo was about nine, like seventy-five per cent of other little girls, she went through a phase of being horse crazy—so did her friend Fanny—and together they thought horses and acted horses all day long.

They stopped walking around, they trotted; they never ran, they either cantered or galloped. Jumps were erected in the garden and round and round they went in an endless gymkhana of jumps and gallops. It was all a pretty harmless amusement, but when they started answering us by neighs and whinnies, it became very trying on the nerves to say the least of it.

They began a wearing-down campaign of persuading us to buy a pony. We held out firmly, pointing out that we could keep two cows on the pasture it took to keep one horse.

"But you're not even using all the fields you've got!' they pointed out, not unreasonably.

"Who's going to look after it?" we countered, although we knew the answer before we asked.

"We are, of course!" they chorused.

And then one day they came to us with shining eyes—they had heard of a pony for sale in Guernsey.

"A little bay mare called Star," they chanted.

There was no doubt but that the phrase had a romantic ring to it. We weakened—even with a feeling of relief—perhaps a real live pony to look after would knock some of the horsy behaviour out of them, and we consented to go and have a look at Star.

A week or so later a couple of delighted small girls were down on the harbour awaiting the arrival of the morning boat. As it drew nearer their excitement knew no bounds, for clearly discernible above the gunwales stood a horsebox. The boat made fast to the quayside and Peter and Philip swung the aged crane out over the boat and secured the dangling hook firmly to the roof of the box, from which now stared the apprehensive eyes of a small bay pony. A few minutes later, the box safely ashore, Fanny and Jo dancing attendance, the pony was led up the hill and into an empty cowshed in the farmyard.

But, regrettably, Star was not a success. She had seemed a quiet biddable animal when we had seen her in Guernsey, but the freedom she enjoyed in Herm as distinct from the stabled life she had become accustomed to lead, went to her head and she showed herself as high-spirited and difficult to handle.

Pat struggled manfully to school her and to teach the children to manage her, but without success, and I, at least, was extremely nervous of an accident. The pony clearly needed more expert handling than we could provide and at last we hit on a compromise. Star was to be sold to a riding school in Guernsey and the two girls should go across twice a week for riding lessons. Fanny and Jo saw the wisdom of this plans and Star was duly sold and underwent a course of intensive schooling. Later, the two girls travelled across each week and the arrangment worked well for a long time.

Some while later the foreman we had at the time on the farm persuaded Peter he needed a working horse. The farmer himself negotiated the buying of it, but when it stepped ashore in Herm I gasped. I could only think of Don Quixote's horse. He was a huge, tall, rangy animal, with ribs and hip-bones sticking out and a lack-lustre coat. He really was a pathetic sight and I was appalled.

"Whatever good will *that* be on the farm?" I wanted to know. "The poor old thing!"

Stan, the farmer who had worked for a greater part of his life among horses, was reassuring.

"You'll not know that horse in a month's time," he avowed.

The horse, which was called Bob, had the air of an elderly gentleman who had fallen on hard times. He picked his way with dignity up the hill behind Stan.

We all came to be fond of Bob. He was quiet and gentle and responded with obvious gratitude to the children's love and attention. Stan was right, after a few weeks in the lush Herm pasture, his coat shone, he filled out and his eyes brightened. He looked a different animal from the one that had walked off the boat so short a while before. His usefulness on the farm was, however, apart from at haymaking time, somewhat in question. He came to spend more and more of his time exclusively with the children—which, because of his staid temperament, suited Peter and me very well. Bob, already old when he came to us, lived for another five years and undoubtedly enjoyed the sunset of his life to the hilt.

Now we have another pony. We gave him to Rosemary for her ninth birthday. He is dappled grey, a crossed Exmoor-New Forest pony, so has, through the winter months, a thick furry coat designed to keep out the chill moorland air. He lives out all the time and thinks nothing of the winters we have in Herm—which, even at their coldest, cannot compare with those he has known on the exposed Exmoor highlands. His name—and it suits him—is Woolly Bear and he soon gave promise of being the fattest, laziest pony in the world. He appeared to have an eating fixation and perpetually cropped the long sweet grass so that we had to lead him into the stable we made for him in the round tower in our garden, just to stop him eating.

We tried putting him with the calves and young heifers

for company, but although they got on famously, the calves showed a regrettable tendency to eat his handsome tail, so we had to separate them—whereupon he started to look dejected and lonely.

But one day Penny saw an advertisement for a baby donkey.

"Wouldn't it be a good idea," she suggested, "to make a paddock next to the house and put Woolly Bear in it so he can't eat as much, and get the baby donkey as a companion for him, because otherwise he'll get so lonely in term time when everyone is away." The idea seemed a good one, and was hailed with approval by everyone. A white post and rail fence was run across a corner of the field adjoining the house and Woolly Bear moved in. He clearly didn't approve too much of his lone existence and stood dejected in the middle of the paddock gazing mournfully around, but the following evening Pandora arrived and was greeted with delight by all of us. She was about seven months old, and stood about as high as a large dog. She had a clearly defined cross on her back, a gingery tinge to her long ears, was fine boned and slender, and was altogether a very pretty little thing. Her introduction to Woolly Bear was a boisterous affair, and we stood by somewhat apprehensively as he chased her madly round and round the paddock. However his exuberance abated after a while, and Pandora was given a bowl of oats and stabled in the round tower for the night. For the first few nights she missed her mother badly, and set up a piteous braying, so that one or other of us was always running out to comfort her and talk to her. It wasn't long, however, before she settled down, and she and Woolly Bear quickly became very good friends. As she grew older, and the nights became warmer, she took to sleeping out, and we have sometimes gone out and shone a torch into the paddock and seen Pandora, legs tucked up beneath her, fast asleep, with Woolly Bear standing protectively above her.

We take Pandora for walks with us around the island, and this she obviously enjoys enormously. For the most part she trots along beside us, but every now and again she rushes off to explore something, and sometimes gets herself tangled up in a clump of brambles, whereupon she sets up a frantic braying and we have to struggle through the thickets to her rescue.

When she was little she enjoyed the freedom of the house, and quickly learned where the kitchen was, so that it was no strange sight to us—though a little startling to visitors—to see Pandora come wheeling in and up to the table in search of any titbits that might be going.

Mimosa, however, is not to be counted among her friends and admirers, and regards her with more than a little trepidation, which is no wonder as Pandora likes nothing better than to chase her.

As with us, the year divides itself into two parts for Woolly Bear and Pandora. A summer half, when there is always someone on hand to lean over the garden wall and stroke their velvety noses and talk to them, and when Woolly resignedly forsakes the idle life and trots amiably round the island with whoever cares to ride him, and the winter half when alone with his friend Pandora he resumes his leisurely life of eating and contemplation.

30

Island Wedding

Most summers on Herm have their share of romances and I don't think any season has come to an end without at least two engagements to the island's credit. These are usually among the young staff who come to the island just for the summer season to help us in the beach cafes or shops, or the hotel. But one summer there was much delighted speculation when Barbara, the niece of John the gardener and his wife Mary, became engaged to David, the engineer on the *Arrowhead*. A Herm wedding at last.

The wedding was planned for October and all were invited. Rosemary, who was 6 years old at the time, was asked to be a bridesmaid, and she was ecstatic at the thought. Never having had occasion to wear so much as a party dress before, it was as big an occasion in her life as it had been for us to be presented to the Queen.

Because of the large number of relatives living in Guernsey it was decided that the wedding would be at the parish church in Saint Peter Port. This presented problems, or if not exactly problems, at least considerable cause for anxiety. What if it was too rough to get across on the day? It was, after all, the season when one might at any time expect the equinoctial gales.

We all felt deeply involved and concerned, but Mary remained unperturbed.

"It will be a fine calm day," she averred. "There is always a spell of two or three nice days around then."

Her faith was justified. Not only was it fine and still, but it was glassy calm and a brilliant sun shone from a cloudless sky. What a wedding day! At ten o'clock the entire population of the island gathered on the quay, all resplendent in our best clothes wth flowers in our buttonholes, and then along the lane from Fisherman's Cottage came the bride—the little three-wheeled motorised truck we used for delivering stores about the island had been transformed into a bridal carriage with white satin ribbons and gaily floating streamers. Sitting in state in the back of the open truck was the bride, her lovely dress spread around her and her veil fluttering gently in the soft breeze. It was an enchanting picture.

The *Arrowhead* bedecked with ribbons and flowers drew in to the quay and the bride, accompanied by Rosemary, beaming delightedly in her pretty, long white dress and chaplet of rosebuds, stepped on board followed by us all.

Rupert looked back as the boat drew away from the harbour and, in accents of dismay, cried, "Oh poor Herm! It's never been left all alone before!" And neither it had, certainly not since our arrival at any rate.

After the ceremony in Guernsey the wedding party returned to Herm and, in true French fashion, the celebrations continued far into the following day.

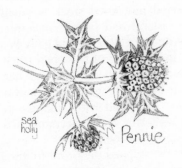

sea holly

Pennie

31

Daffodils

After the failure of the pottery we decided to concentrate our efforts during the winter months on yet another island industry which we had already begun in an experimental way in the field by Fisherman's Cottage—that of flower growing.

We were pleased with the quality of the flowers we were able to grow and felt that we could well increase our efforts in this direction. To some extent in flower growing one is producing goods from an island source of supply because, although it is true that there is a considerable outlay of capital in the first instance to buy an initial stock of bulbs, thereafter they multiply and in three years have doubled themselves.

We consulted John, the gardener, who is a Guernseyman and had been a grower of flowers and vegetables on a commercial scale all his life. John was enthusiastic but pointed out that the existing field at Fisherman's was too small for any large-scale effort and he chose another site on the top of the island where there were two adjacent fields sheltered by a pine wood from the east wind, open to the south and sloping gently to the west.

The tractor moved in and prepared the ground and the following autumn we planted several tons of daffodil bulbs and as many iris.

Unbelievably early by English standards the first green shoots pierced the ground—we watched them grow until, by Christmas, they stood several inches from the ground.

Towards the end of February, buds were beginning to appear and by early March picking began. Until I actually began to pick daffodils I had imagined it would be a most pleasant task. With thoughts of Wordsworth's "Host of golden daffodils . . . fluttering and dancing in the breeze", I saw myself delighting in the task, with armfuls of lovely fragrant blooms. It wasn't at all like that. To begin with you don't pick them in flower. When the bud appears it is pointing vertically upwards; gradually, over a period of a day or two, it descends to the horizontal and picking begins when it is just past this point and before it opens.

Daffodils are heavy held in the crook of the arm and it is an arm-aching, back-breaking job. Moreover, it is a wet and sticky one, and it is necessary to wear a heavy rubber overall or you would soon be soaked through. Some people are allergic to this sticky juice that exudes from the broken stems, and it brings them out in a rash so that they have to protect their hands with gloves.

After picking, the flowers are stacked in buckets of water in a warm shed and here they soon open. Then bunching begins.

John's wife, Mary, proved to be an expert buncher and she instructed the rest of us how to arrange the flowers, secure the stems with two elastic bands and pack them in boxes. She organised us into a production line and we quickly learnt to be deft at our particular task. Generally speaking the men do the picking and the women and girls the bunching and packing. Sometimes in the height of the

161

seaon work will go on well into the early hours of the morning so as to get the boxes off on the first boat next day, when they are taken down the hill piled in the trailer of the tractor to be loaded on to the boat and taken to Guernsey for shipment to England. They are at Covent Garden the following morning, and it always gives me a thrill to see the boxes all labelled "Herm Island Flowers" on the lid and to think that these same flowers will so soon find their way on to London streets and into London homes.

After the daffodil harvest comes the iris and the procedure is much the same, although in this case the flower has to be cut with a sharp knife instead of picked by hand. In certain weather conditions iris can suffer from a particular blight called botritis which marks the petals with a disfiguring black spot so that every flower has to be carefully scrutinised for the telltale blemish and discarded if it appears.

The flower market is a strange one and so many circumstances affect the sale of the flowers that it is almost impossible to say until the season is at an end and the last flower box dispatched whether it has been a good or a bad one. What applies one year may well not apply the next; if one's flowers appear to be exceptionally early, well, so may everyone else's be and the markets will be glutted and the price low; but if, on the other hand, everyone else's are early and yours, for some reason, late or vice versa, then the price is very much in your favour. One year our flowers were very early compared to most people's and the price being paid was high, and then there was a heavy fall of snow in England preventing the lorries getting through to Covent Garden—there was no buying and the price was non-existent. On the other hand, at the time of Queen Mary's death, which was in the very early days of our flower growing, the price suddenly soared, especially for purple flowers.

We continued to grow flowers for many years, and in many respects it suited the island economy—providing work and bringing in money at an otherwise slack time of the year, but nevertheless, it had its problems, the chief one being that of labour during the picking and bunching season. Early March is a time of increasing activity and pressure on the island as we prepare to open up the hotel, the shops and catering businesses, and each season saw us more and more hard pressed to achieve this smoothly, when almost every available person was engaged with the flowers. We studied the receipts from flower production. One good year tended to cloud our realisation of the fact that the prices we had got over the years had fluctuated greatly, so that we had in fact not done much more than break even, and we came to the conclusion that we would do better to concentrate our effort in preparing the island for the tourist season ahead and hand over the flower fields to the quickly expanding farm which could be expected to more than compensate us through milk production. A decision which proved to be undoubtedly a right one. The two fields are, in their turn, now strip fed to over ninety head of cattle and a useful hay crop is taken off them every year.

32

Peter the Post

Although Guernsey has its own government the postal services were operated by the British Government and before the last war there was a small G.P.O. on Herm. After the war, and during his short tenancy, Mr. Jefferies approached the Post Office and asked them if they would re-establish this facility. This they declined to do, which meant that the people living in Herm would have to go to Guernsey to post a letter. This was obviously an impossible situation and so Mr. Jefferies, with the approval of the British Post Office, decided to provide for the small community then living on Herm what the postal authorities refused to do, a local postal service, and to print his own stamps.

Each postal packet would of course have to have the appropriate British Post Office stamp on it to take it onwards from Guernsey, but the Herm stamp performed the service of taking the packets to Guernsey and there posting it. A truly local mail carrying service in fact and one which was clearly necessary.

This had hardly been established when Peter and I took over but the first set of stamps had been printed. The Post Office reacted immediately to the design and bitterly resented the use of the word "postage" which appeared on all the stamps. The carrying of post, they said, was their prerogative. So in effect they were saying, "We won't carry it, you can, but you musn't say so!"

Out came the word "postage" from the design and the first Herm stamp has a big empty space at the bottom.

Another cause for grievance was the use of the word 'stamp'. In all our correspondence and in conversation with the British Postal authorities they always heavily referred to what *we* called Herm stamps as "Herm carriage labels". Neither Peter nor I felt very strongly about which name they were called, but after all the word stamp is shorter, and everyone knows what a stamp is and does whereas the other term is not so familiar.

When we took over we realised the carrying of mail was a serious responsibility. Peter drew up regulations to safeguard its security and used only locked mailbags, the sorting office in Guernsey having one key and we the other.

It is not possible to say accurately how many pieces of mail we carried each year but it was certainly in the region of between 150,000 and 200,000 pieces. The stamps quickly began to create interest in philatelic circles, and letters started to come in from all over the world enquiring about them.

I appointed myself postmistress and answered all the letters myself, and as a result, developed quite an interest in stamp collecting. I had no idea what a many-faceted business it was and how time consuming it could be. I found I was spending more and more time answering letters, but it was interesting interesting work and I enjoyed it.

I began by working at the correspondence at home, but as the volume of business grew this soon became impracticable —we had not the space in the house to give over a room to the work, and I spent a large proportion of my time setting the work out and putting it away again out of the reach of small marauding hands. Stamps have to be carefully filed according to their various denominations and issue, or else chaos ensues—moreover, they have to be stored interleaved with waxed paper and in completely dry conditions, or else they stick together and wastage occurs. The net result of all this being that quite a lot of space needs to be given over to them and filing cabinets and damp-proof cupboards provided.

Across the garden was an outbuilding attached to the

farm, and this was converted without too much labour and expense into an office for me, where, in between the claims of the children and the cooking stove, I could work undisturbed at the stamps.

From time to time we produced new definitive issues which were in use for several years, and every now and again a commemorative stamp to record some historic occasion. The preparation of an issue of stamps is no mean task, and to do it in under six months is almost impossible unless one spends every moment of one's time on it. Firstly there is the subject to be chosen and research to be carried out as philatelists are quick to pounce on any inaccuracy which might appear in the design. When we produced an issue featuring Neolithic man we were involved in much more research than we had at first bargained for. What did the island look like four thousand years ago? and for that matter, what did Neolithic man look like? What implements did he use to hunt with, fish with? The research was lengthy and had to be painstaking before the designer could go to work.

In 1952 a delightful old Guernseyman, the Reverend S. T. Percival, designed a coat of arms for the island of Herm, and this we adopted as the theme for another definitive issue.

An article headed "The Arms Of Herm", which appeared in *The Coat of Arms*, a magazine brought out by the Heraldry Society, describes the arms thus: "Azure on a bend or between 2 dolphins embowed argent 3 monks cowled and habited sable." It symbolises the golden island set in its azure sea and its long history as a monastic settlement.

The preparation of the Churchill issue which we brought out in 1965 to commemorate the twentieth anniversary of the liberation of the islands and in memory of that great man was the one that appealed especially to me for very personal reasons. The stamp bore the likeness of Sir Winston Churchill, together with the words, "Our dear Channel Islands", which was the expression he had used during the war when referring to these islands where Peter and I have since made our home. Moreover, we had pin-pointed the two places where my brother Geoffrey had been O.C. of raids carried out against the Germans: the Casquets Lighthouse, where he had removed the German crew, and Dixcart Bay, Sark, where he had landed and taken prisoners.

I remember how when home on leave he had pored over old family photographs and ciné films taken in Sark when we were children. We weren't to know why at the time but understood when later we read about the raid in the newspapers. After this particular episode he had been summoned to the Prime Minister and had personally told Mr. Churchill about the raid. For his part in these Channel Island raids and many others into German occupied France he was awarded the D.S.O., M.C., and Bar. He was killed over Sicily later in the war. All of this we felt provided a very special family link, not only with the occasion commemorated by the stamp, but also with our wartime leader.

And then suddenly we brought out a particular issue, which, because of a set of freak circumstances, turned out to be a best seller—it was quite unexpected and we were dumbfounded by the number of enquiries and demands there were for this particular set of stamps. We were swamped but mustered all our efforts and personnel to help in despatching the orders all over the world.

That year was a good business year, and with this very successful issue at long last we were enabled to shrug off the final repayments of the overdraft that we had arranged when firstly we bought the lease of Herm. The relief was enormous.

Every year we had gradually improved the various little businesses we had developed on the island and each year we had sent our accounts to our bank in England with a long letter explaining them, the year that was past, and how we were going to 'do better' next year. I think that particular branch of our bank where we had first raised the overdraft which had made our island venture possible, being in the heart of a vast northern industrial city, normally engaged in financing purely manufacturing industrial developments, must have had a soft spot for our little green island set in the midst of its blue, diamond-studded sea, for we never met our repayment targets, but each year our accounts came back with a friendly, encouraging letter.

At last, however, we had struggled out of this position. Overdrafts are, I know, a quite proper and necessary part of business, but this one had often given us sleepless nights.

Thankfully we unleashed the albatross from about our necks and breathed freely for the first time for years.

And then a series of events occurred which looked most promising to us. Guernsey along with the other self governing Queen Dependencies such as the Isle of Man and Jersey were offered the right to take over the running of their own Post Office from the British Government. Naturally we thought that as we had operated a mail service for more than twenty years with the knowledge and tacit approval of the British Post Office, we would continue to do so but under the umbrella of the Guernsey Post Office Board instead of the British Post Office. Clearly this would be a good thing and much of the interest stimulated by the Guernsey 'take-over' would, we hoped, rub off on us. Thus, like quite a few other islands in the world and for that matter, small countries as well, by the help of our stamps, we would be able to balance our budget—in our case, set off all public-service expenses and the multitudinous small costs which mount up to massive sums in maintaining an island and its community.

Full of high hopes we decided to produce a new definitive issue of stamps to come out at the time of the change over. We chose as the theme ships which had carried mail between the islands and mainlands of, firstly Normandy and then England from the eleventh century to modern times.

The authorities in Guernsey gave their permission for the set and approval to the design but, like the British Post Office when they had objected to the word "postage", would not countenance the use of the word "mail". The expression must be "Ships which had maintained communications between the Islands".

We chose a designer and printer in London and went ahead, and then the hammer blow fell, suddenly and unexpectedly. The Guernsey Post Office Board brought out a law which said in effect that anyone using what purported to be a stamp other than a Guernsey Post Office stamp on an envelope or packet and posted it, would after the day they took over from the British Government be fined £500 on each occasion.

Fearing that a local issue within the Bailiwick could damage their image as an issuing authority they were determined to rub us out of existence. We didn't agree with them and did everything in our power to persuade them to permit us to continue, but it was not to be.

The production of our ship issue was well in hand, too late to cancel, so we were very worried as to what to do. The cost we had already incurred was very considerable; should we cut our losses or carry on and bring out the issue, even though we would only be able to use them for a matter of a week or two? We decided on the latter course and the stamps came out on 17th September 1969 and their use had to be discontinued on 1st October. So on 30th September 1969 Herm local stamps were used for the last time.

Some philatelic journals and newspapers had commented on the decision not to allow the service to continue, so during that fortnight when the last issue of Herm local stamps were in service many thousands of postal packets were carried, especially on the last day. In philatelic circles first-day covers are an especially prized collector's item, whereas a last-day cover is most unusual. It was a sad day for us, and for many hundreds of collectors of Herm local stamps all over the world. In an age where individuality is stifled more and more, this seemed like just another example of the dead hand of conformity wiping out a colourful, interesting little business. The situation was in no way lightened for us by the thought that on 1st October a real genuine sub-post office was to open on Herm Island with Peter in the role of sub-postmaster!

Now after more than two years we are finding, and it is some small consolation, that philatelists who used to be collectors of Herm stamps write to us for first-day covers of the new, and we must admit, very attractive Guernsey stamps because they want the "Herm Island" cancellation mark on the envelope.

33

A New Lease

Throughout the years the seven-year break clause in our lease of the island from the States of Guernsey, continued to rile us. Our accounts showed a distressing situation. The small businesses we ran, the beach cafés and the hotel, the farm, the shop and tavern, each individually made a profit, but when these profits were set against the enormous costs of maintaining the island as a whole they were swamped. The subvention we received from the poll tax made but a small contribution towards these costs. We must expand the little businesses, and yet how dare we infuse more of our capital into the island, when our security of tenure was so short lived? Still less, how could we raise a capital loan elsewhere? Yet expand we must, or go under.

The terms of our lease demanded that the island must at all times be neat and tidy, with well-maintained paths and, indeed, since it was our home, we wouldn't have had it otherwise; but as more and more people came to the island, it became increasingly expensive to do this. We found we had to employ men whose sole jobs were to attend to these tasks. We had to erect public lavatories and maintain them. Whereas, we fully accepted that the cost of running the island boat and the electrical supply, both extremely expensive items, was our liability, it seemed to us inequitable that any part of those expenses which would normally be borne by the State, such as road maintenance and clearage, sewage disposal, public conveniences and water supply, should come out of our pockets. We pay all Guernsey taxes but do not receive all the benefits therefrom. To us it seemed right and proper that the whole of the receipts from the poll tax and not just a part of them should come to us as a contribution to these public service costs. Also the method of assessing our rent involving, as it did, a complicated study of our accounts, was proving to be a cumbersome and time-wasting business from everybody's point of view, theirs and ours, and one which clearly none of us liked. And so in the spring of 1962 we again approached the States of Guernsey asking them to reconsider the terms of the lease. It was a lengthy affair but ended satisfactorily so far as the period of the lease went. It now runs to the year 2029.

With the new financial clauses, however, we were not so pleased, particularly as regards the revenue to be found for public services. This was determined on a descending scale and we were forced to the decision to try and keep all island and public services down to a minimum— which was not the healthiest of situations and could only have the result of making the island look slightly 'tatty'. In the event, however, we found we could not bring ourselves to follow this cheese-paring policy and year by year the cost of keeping the island tidy and clean, and of public services generally, mounted.

We redoubled our efforts to make the returns from the various businesses more realistic, and now that we had an unbroken sixty-six years of the lease in front of us we decided to infuse more of our capital into it.

First on the list came Belvoir bay beach hut, and the first requirement here was that we should enlarge the terrace which we had made over ten years before, so that it could accommodate a larger hut. In order to do so Peter had once again to make arrangements to ship a bulldozer across on a barge towed behind a couple of launches. Always a spectacular sight, the operation was watched by most of us. From a distance it is not easy to see the barge because it floats so low in the water, so the two launches pulling it have all the appearance of being pursued over the waves by a monster red bulldozer. Very incongruous! Landing, if not exactly split-second timing is certainly set within very narrow time margins

172

as the top of the barge must be as level as possible with the lower end of the slipway to enable a smooth run-off.

Once arrived at Belvoir bay the bulldozer made short work of moving back the face of the cliff and of levelling out a larger platform. We put on order an attractive pavilion-style prefabricated hut from England and when it arrived the various wooden sections were taken by tractor and trailer over the hill and assembled in a pile at the top of the steep slope immediately above the bay.

Jimmie, the Scottish mason, was working below on the site and Peter called him up to see the sections and to discuss the erection and actual siting of the hut. Each section appeared to be a four-man load and Peter left after a while promising to send over the necessary men that same afternoon. When he returned with his labour force it was to find that Jimmie had carried the entire load, piece by piece, alone and single handed down to the site. He had apparently shouldered the sections on his back, a truly formidable feat, and, looking at the large pavilion assembled there today, it is almost impossible to imagine how he did it.

Another obvious point for development was the shop. In size it had virtually remained unchanged since the early days when we had opened it to sell shellware, although we had increased the variety and character of the stock and now sold a number of gifts of one kind and another.

We were beginning to get requests for French perfumes and Continental jewellery and beach clothes. It was impossible to handle such a range in the tiny little shop as it was and we decided on a fairly large-scale development.

Between the shop, which was housed in the old boat store, and the Mermaid Cottages, there was a steeply sloping stretch of rough ground of about half an acre in extent. It was overgrown with rank grass, bramble and scrub, and we selected this place for our extension development, being quite sure that whatever we built there, if carefully and attractively planned, far from detracting from the appearance of the island would, in fact, greatly enhance the scene and would help to consolidate the little village around the harbour. When the bulldozer had finished at Belvoir we directed its activities to this area and soon we had a flat, simple building site, cleared of all boulders and undergrowth which, like an artist's canvas, stood ready and waiting for whatever we chose to build there.

Peter sketched his ideas on his drawing board and I was thrilled when I saw what was in his mind. He pictured a group of miniature buildings built on small cobbled terraces of different levels. There were pantiled walls and deep-set arches, small bowfronted shop windows with hanging baskets of flowers and, as a centre piece to this fantasy, a pigeon cote housing white doves and surrounded by climbing roses.

The Mermaid Tavern was another place where we could with advantage improve the facilities and we decided upon a verandah extension which would be open fronted with a wide overhanging roof supported on pit props washed up by the sea and mounted on a low red tile-topped wall. This would more than double the effective space of the building, besides looking attractive and taking away the rather flat appearance the front had had before. We decided the garden would be greatly improved by building a high sheltering wall on the seaward side. This would complete the walled garden effect we were anxious to provide as the Mermaid itself ran along one side, the Long Barn snack bar along the fourth side by a thick hedge of euonymus and roses.

The whole of the front of the village area was served by a dusty narrow path running from the old boat store at present being used as the only shop, to the Mermaid. The path passed within a few feet of the Mermaid Cottages, which we used as additional bedrooms to the hotel, and, quite apart from the lack of privacy, these rooms were frequently subjected to swirls of dust blowing in through the windows. Although we couldn't possibly convince ourselves that any work we did to improve this state of affairs would be directly revenue producing we couldn't resist the temptation, while so much other work was being put in hand in the vicinity, of making the effort. Peter decided to move the path 20 feet forward from the front of the cottages and at the same time to widen it.

For the last few years we had become conscious of a growing demand amongst our daily visitor population for more substantial meals than our snack bar or beach huts could provide. We had dealt with this by opening up a non-resident trade in our hotel dining-room, but at peak periods of the year this would become sorely overcrowded, and not only the dining-room, but the lounge and small bar as well. This seemed to be an appropriate time to rectify this situation. Between the hotel and a couple of cottages in the village was a courtyard which we used as a stores yard as it backed on to the kitchen. We decided to remove this activity to the rear of the hotel and to convert this yard into a restaurant which would be additional to the hotel dining-room and would deal exclusively with daily visitors.

This time we consulted a London architect who specialised in restaurant architecture. Again Peter had some very definite ideas in mind and, somewhat to my surprise, for I had rather imagined architects liked a free rein to their creativeness, he faithfully interpreted Peter's dreams and schemes. As always, I had the greatest difficulty in visualising from the plans the three-dimensional building which would eventually materialise and I must have sorely tried their patience when my opinion was asked about this and that. It was all the more confusing to visualise from a flat drawing because the flooring and also the ceiling were to be of three different levels, but when a year or so later it was at last completed I was full of admiration that Peter could have devised such an interesting and unusual room. Not only were the levels of floor and ceiling different but their treatment was varied by the use of different types and colour of wood. The restaurant, though large, and capable of seating 120 people, is entered through one of the original cottages and so in no way spoils the appearance of the village. Two of the pillars supporting the roof inside the restaurant were specially placed so as to house between them a very fine model of a passenger cargo steamship, 1915 vintage, which used to carry passengers across the Red Sea to Jidda for their Mecca pilgrimage and which Peter had discovered a year or two before in a ship

175

chandler's in Weymouth; but when the time came to take it down the hill and put it *in situ,* as a family we found that we had become much too attached to it to allow it to leave its 'temporary' resting place in our house and there it still is to this day. However, it did at least give its name to the restaurant, which we call 'The Ship'.

Yet another piece of work which we decided to put in hand that same winter was the provision of more adequate staff quarters for the men we employed through the six months of the summer season. The girl staff were all housed fairly satisfactorily in the manor house at the top of the hill, which over the years we had tidied up and improved, adding bathrooms and recreational facilities. But the men were in much need of improved conditions. We decided to take the roof off the kitchen which was a one-storeyed building 90 feet by 30 feet standing along the back of the hotel. By raising the roof and adding a new floor we would achieve the new accommodation we were looking for.

And then, having our plans made, we turned our minds to the very thorny problem of how we were going to set about achieving it all, how to convert these exciting looking plans and schemes into reality. It represented an enormous amount of work. Where and how could we possibly get together a work force adequate to the task? We knew how difficult it was to obtain labour locally, and then Peter had an inspiration. He thought of the last years of the war when he had been in Italy and had got to know and like the Northern Italians and had admired their cheerful industry and amazing skill and artistry in building. Within a fortnight Peter and I were on our way to Italy.

Combining business with a high percentage of pleasure we headed for Santa Margharita on the Ligurian coast and settled down to enjoy a holiday while we thought out a plan of campaign.

Santa Margharita is a lovely sun-soaked spot built round a fascinating harbour, and there we found a hotel whose garden, full of roses, lilies and lizards, rambled down to the sea and a rocky cove where the swimming was superb. From Santa

Margharita a coastal road winds round the steep indented coast to lovely Porto Fino, where we would drive each evening and dine on the quayside watching the beautiful yachts at anchor, their lights mirrored in the dark still water, and admire the careless beauty of the houses, churches and campaniles climbing up the steep hillside and clustering round the port.

We were in no hurry to get to grips with our task, but at last Peter said we had better think about driving north to one of the industrial cities where we could visit the bureau of commerce and enquire about available labour.

In fact we didn't do anything of the sort. We had phenomenal luck. Peter approached the concierge of the hotel where we were staying to ask his advice about which town would be likely to provide the happiest hunting ground for our purpose, explaining to him the nature of the work we wanted to do. His reply was immediate and astonishing.

"But I have an uncle who is a master builder and I think he would be very interested in your scheme. He has his own team of workers, all craftsmen in their trade. Work is scarce for builders in Italy just now and I think they would go with my uncle to your island."

He volunteered to contact his uncle and to put the whole thing to him. Peter and I continued our holiday and Roberto, the concierge, duly contacted his Uncle Bruno.

There was indeed a period of recession in Italy at that time and many tradesmen, the building profession in particular, were having a thin time of it. The prospect of an offer of nine months' employment was an attractive one which appealed instantly to Uncle Buno. It was arranged that he should fly over to Guernsey a week or so after our return to discuss on the site the plans we had in mind, and which were now with an architect in Guernsey, being knocked into shape.

But what about their wives and families, I wanted to know. Would the men want to leave them for so long a time? Peter explained that there was a tradition in Italy of exporting labour. The men were accustomed to leaving home in search of work. Indeed we had noticed ourselves how Italians were

177

being employed on road-making, dam building and on the construction of vast hydro-electric installations all over Europe. They would sometimes be away from their homes for years at a time, sending home money to support their wives and families.

We returned home and a week or two later Uncle Bruno arrived. He was a short, rotund little man with dancing brown eyes. He spoke no word of English but possessed a lively determination to communicate with us just the same. Peter had a smattering of Italian and Bruno spoke some French, though we were somewhat bemused by his Italian accent when he spoke it, and he, no doubt, by our English one. Still we managed fairly well and after seeing what we had in mind it was arranged that Bruno would return with his work team at the beginning of October, by which time Peter would have the detailed plans drawn up and all would be ready to start work, the summer visitors would have all departed and we would have room to house the men.

The only thing about the arrangement that seriously worried us was the business of communication and, although we had managed to talk and discuss the work on broad principles, we were fairly certain we should run into difficulties when it came to the detailed interpretation of the plans. And then we thought of Jill.

Jill was an old friend of ours. She had first holidayed on the island some years before and had then returned for several consecutive summers and worked the season on the island. For the last two or three years, however, she had been employed by a travel agency as a courier in Italy. She spoke fluent Italian. We could think of no one we would rather have to help us as an interpreter if she were free to come. She was, and promised to arrive at the beginning of October.

On the evening of 10th October we were all waiting at Rosiere landing. As the boat approached, over the water came the sound of singing and as they came alongside and, headed by Bruno, stepped ashore, it seemed as if they transformed Herm into a small part of their native land, so vibrant and alive was the atmosphere they generated.

178

We housed them in the Mermaid Cottages and fed them in the Tavern adjoining, and the whole area took on the atmosphere of an Italian village. In the evening they played cards or stood outside leaning against the wall, smoking and talking among themselves. They were a friendly, amiable crew with ready smiles and a *"Buon giorno"* for any who passed, and always there was the sound of singing, gay and lilting or haunting and sad.

The island children were never far from the scene of their activities, and the Italians adored them and spoilt them abominably. They made them all brown paper fore and aft caps like the ones they wore themselves and wrote their names on the brim, they fed them with sweets and never did they go across to Guernsey but they returned with a little present for each child.

Their industry was heartwarming to see. They started at first light and were still at work long after dusk had fallen, working by the light of lamps slung from the trees. Their ability to work hard was prodigious and, thanks to Jill and her powers of interpretation, communication was never a stumbling block, although she found she had to acquire a hitherto unused vocabulary of technical terms, and to this end we supplied her with an Italian builder's manual.

The work progressed apace. The first task they engaged upon was the construction of a massive granite retaining wall below the platform we had bulldozed out ready for the two new shops. It was fascinating to notice how their own artistic temperament was evident in all they did.

It was Angelo who thought of collecting the many coloured pebbles off the beach and pressing them into the cement between the granite slabs of the walls to give them texture and a sea wall appearance, Roberto who swept his pallet backwards and forwards over the plaster on the shop walls, producing a rippling effect of light and shade and taking away the flat look, and it was Luigi who showed us how to produce the lovely sun-kissed burnt sienna colour they use so much in Italy and which looked so right against the vivid blue of sea and sky.

179

In the high granite wall surrounding the Mermaid garden they built a semi-circular archway similar to many old arch ways we have seen in Guernsey, but gave it, and the other walls they built too, a Mediterranean quality by topping them with red pantiles. Unrequested by Peter, but utterly charming, was the circular picture window which made its appearance in a high wall adjoining the new Ship Restaurant and which gives to the little courtyard behind it an entrancing view of the sweep of the beach from the harbour to Fisherman's Cottage.

Some buildings we painted a Pompeian pink and yet another, a warm honeydew melon shade. It all looked very gay and colourful when at last it was finished and it reflected the warm, gay nature of those who had built it.

The English *signorina* Jill became a firm favourite with them all and when, a year later, she was next in Italy and visited the village where most of them lived, she was made much of and fêted from house to house, and it was insisted that she meet their wives, their numerous children and indeed, most of their friends and relations.

It was May when they left us and we were sad to see them go—so, I think, were they, and we have promised to seek their help again when next we have a large-scale project on our hands. We cannot say when that will be—but that it will be is to some extent or other inevitable.

It has always been annoying to us when people have said, "You must *never* commercialise Herm—it is so lovely and it would spoil it so." Such people seem to forget that Herm is our home and we are the last people to want to spoil it, but commercialise it we must if we are to continue to live here. One cannot support a community of people on lovely scenery, and there is no reason to suppose that development cannot go hand in hand with natural beauty. Both Peter and I firmly believe this and bear this fact in mind in all that we attempt to do.

34

Farming

To both Peter and I one of the more satisfying aspects to life
on Herm has been the farm. Ever since possessing that first
field at College Farm in Linton, to have had a stake in the
land has been basically gratifying to us.

To begin with, Peter and Philip looked after the farm on
Herm between them. Both had a certain amount of
knowledge—admittedly based more on sheep farming from
their early upbringing in New Zealand than cattle, although
Philip had spent some months on a ranch in British Columbia
before the war, but both knew how to milk, a certain amount
about feeding and were experienced at driving a tractor.

There were only six cows and for a time they managed.
However, with so many other island affairs to attend to, it was
clearly impracticable for them to continue doing the work
themselves, especially as we wished to increase the scope of
the farm, and so after a while we took on a farm foreman,
although Peter continued to lay down the policy to be

employed. This was, in fact, very simple, and still is, as we decided to grow nothing but grass, bring back as many fields into good heart as we could and keep as many cows as the available pasture would warrant.

We used to artificially inseminate the cows and many a morning we would be knocked up by the foreman with a request to get the inseminator across as soon as possible. Time and tide were frequently against us and the whole exercise proved to be expensive and impracticable. We keep our own bulls now: Philibuster, though it was suggested that a more appropriate name for him would be Henry VIII since he has so many wives; and Crusader of the Spurs, still a youngster, who has the makings of a very fine bull indeed. In the summer they are put out to graze on a 20-foot chain tether fixed around their horns, through their nose rings, and then on to a peg driven into the ground in a field adjoining our garden. There they stand in the long grass under the trees, obviously delighting in the fresh air and sun, a welcome change from their bull pens in the farmyard. They have both learnt the trick of lowering their heads, swinging their tethers backwards and forwards and finally, with an expert flick, getting the chain hitched round their horns so that it lies down the length of their back. Then they move their massive heads so that the chain rubs up and down and scratches their back—whereupon, a dreamy expression comes over their faces and they stand endlessly engaged in this activity.

Sometimes our involvement with farming affairs has been of a somewhat dramatic nature. One quiet Sunday afternoon we were sitting in the garden when we became aware of a great commotion on the other side of the garden wall. Hurrying round we saw an astonishing sight. In the huge solid granite drinking trough to the side of the lane lay a cow, on its back, its four legs waving frantically in the air. The cowman was completely at a loss. He explained that she had been jostled by another cow and had overbalanced into the trough. It was an incredibly tight fit and the cow was incapable of helping herself, and because of her thrashing

182

legs, the cowman was equally unable to help her.

And then John, the gardener, turned up. John is a Guernseyman and is ever resourceful in almost any eventuality—almost any situation, however bizarre, apparently had its parallel during the Occupation. Such appeared to be the case now. Long planks of wood were fetched and levered under the animal until eventually she could be rolled out sideways.

Recently another action-packed incident occured. A visiting tourist had left a gate open in a field and many of the young heifers had got out. On retrieving them one was found to be missing. A search was organised, and about midday Benjamin ran into the house to say that the heifer had been found. She had, he said, fallen down a shaft in a spur of woodland adjoining the field. Peter went with him and discovered that what had happened was that she had fallen through the ground into an underground tunnel, the existence of which we had been quite unaware. The tunnel was steep, and the heifer had slithered down backwards and come to rest about 50 feet down, where the tunnel levelled out. She was just visible when Peter lay flat on his stomach and peered down, but appeared to be making no effort to climb back out. Peter called for a couple of ropes, and, securing one round his ankle, he was lowered head first down the sloping shaft. He admits to being not a little apprehensive about his possible reception by the frightened heifer at the other end. Luckily, however, she was entirely co-operative, and seemed to realise that something was being done to help her. Peter was able to secure the second rope around her neck. Then Peter was hauled out backwards, gently pulling the heifer with him—though, unfortunately, she was exhilarated at sensing release and scrambled out the last few yards over Peter's chest, much bruising it in the process. We were all thankful to have found the poor beast, who might have languished there for much longer before being discovered, or, indeed, remained undiscovered and died there.

The tunnel remains a mystery to us, and where it leads to we do not know. There has always been a legend that there is a tunnel running from approximately this place right up into the manor buildings, and perhaps this is it; but as it seems to be highly unsafe to venture along it we shall not be exploring it yet awhile.

There is a rumour that on Herm there is buried treasure belonging to the church and hidden by the monks when they were being harried by the Protestants in the sixteenth century. We are always hopeful that we'll stumble on it, and one day we thought that we had quite literally done exactly that. Philip was probing around in the undergrowth on a steep bank near the harbour to site a flight of steps, when he caught his foot in something and came hurtling down dragging with him a large metal object. On inspection it was found to be a big silver tray, in the upraised handle of which Philip had caught his foot. Poking around further we discovered a small underground bricked chamber and in it two more pieces, salvers, about 8 inches across. We were very excited. But alas, the small bricked chamber turned out to be nothing more romantic than the cesspit of a nearby cottage, and the salvers, though handsome enough to look at, are plated silver, and of little more than intrinsic value. The large tray, however, has been put into service in the hotel and looks very splendid when carried into the dining-room arrayed with dressed lobster or crabs. How it came to find its way into a dis-used cesspit we shall never know, and as for the real buried treasure, the island so far has refused to give up her secret.

We have two brothers taking care of the farm now, Mike and Maurice, and over the years the herd has grown so that now we have over ninety head of cattle, and those fields that we use are in good heart and look trim and orderly. Each year we reclaim more of the island, and it is a source of enormous pleasure and contentment to Peter and me to see cattle grazing on land which, a comparatively short time ago, was infested by rabbits and covered by impenetrable bramble and scrub. Although we have had a milking machine for many years now, we plan a new up-to-date layout in the farmyard which will enable us to milk up to sixty cows in just over an hour. All our surplus milk goes

The Shopping Piazza which the Italians built.

The Mermaid Cottages 1949 where we first stayed.

Beginning work on the front of the Mermaid Cottages and Gift shops.

Mermaid Cottages and shopping Piazza (looking N.).

Ben, Rosemary, Pennie and Rupert on a wet winter's day on the
Spine Road, 1958.

The family, Summer 1959.

The Manor House
as we first saw it.

The Manor House
reconstruction,
1957; the Church
in the background.

The Manor today.

to Guernsey on the *Henry Rose's* first trip in the morning, and we are currently sending up to 150 gallons over daily.

Our farm is blessed with, by Channel Island standards, large fields, some of 8 acres or more. The local measure of land is the vergee of which there are 2½ to the acre, and our farm, when we have recovered all the farm lands, will be upwards of 300 vergees (120 acres). The advantages which these large fields gives us is, however, largely offset by the costs of shipping.

We have grown very fond of the Guernsey breed. They are 'nice' cows, and their warm golden honey colour as they graze across the green sloping fields with a backdrop of heavenly blue sea and long sweeping sandy beaches is a picture beyond compare.

We have often felt we would like to keep bees on Herm, and the thought of a supply of honeycombs for the breakfast table is an attractive one, but there are snags. To begin with we feel fairly sure that it is a specialist operation, about which none of us knows anything, and, secondly, we are advised that it would require keeping a particularly strong, hardy bee—strong enough to fly against the fairly persistent winds we get here and so prevent themselves being blown off the island. We gave permission to a friend in Guernsey to keep some of his bees—they were a hardy black bee—on the island to see how they would do. The experiment was not a great success and I remember for instance that when the bees were found to be swarming in the garden of the cottage next to us we spent fruitless hours putting in telephone calls all over Guernsey trying to find the bee-keeper and then arranging his transport across to Herm to come and take them. Moreover, a black bee is a ferocious bee, and they were distinctly hostile tenants. If any strange noise annoyed them they would fly into a fury and attack whatever caused the noise, so that the farmer driving the tractor was more than once set upon and stung badly. At the end of the agreed term we discontinued the arrangement, and honeycomb, when we have it, must be transported from Saint Peter Port market.

185

We are much plagued by rabbits on the island. Their name is Legion and we have a serious problem in dealing with them. Rabbits have a regrettable tendency to increase in number in direct proportion to the availability of grass, so that the better the farm flourishes, so also do the rabbits. For many years we managed to keep their numbers in control by a vigorous trapping programme during the winter months, and were able to offset the cost of the trappers' wages by selling the rabbits; but in recent years this has not been possible as a law was introduced and passed in Guernsey forbidding the use of gin traps—which we found to be the only effective form of trap.

Our first attempts at shooting them did not begin to answer the problem. It was an expensive method, because of the price of the cartridges and also a shot rabbit is not always a saleable one.

We seriously considered introducing foxes to the island as possibly being of assistance to our problem. We understood them to be avid hunters and visualised them decimating our rabbit population in quite a short while. However, we were to be disillusioned. At the time we were considering this, a book on the wild fox appeared on the market and on reading this we realised that to introduce them to the island would in no way answer our problem. It appears that basically the fox is a very idle fellow, quite disinclined to exert himself to catch rabbits if it involves giving chase and would much prefer to feed by scavenging or plundering a chicken run where his prey is easy to come by. In fact he is capable of coming to terms with the rabbits in the environment of his earth and living quite amicably with them.

A pest to our farming efforts though rabbits are, they nevertheless provide a very welcome addition to our winter larder. Benjamin learnt to shoot when away at prep school. In fact his photo appeared in the *Field* at the time, under the caption "Teach 'em young", showing him shouldering his gun and holding his bag of some dozen rooks or so by the feet. On his thirteenth birthday he asked if he might have a 4.10 cartridge belt. This was so clearly 'a foot in the door' that we were not at all surprised when on the approach of his fourteenth birthday he came up with the request for a 4.10 double-barrelled shotgun. Peter, hoping he might land one that had been tucked away in someone's attic, advertised in the local paper stating that he wanted a gun for a 14-year-old boy who would cherish and value it. We had no replies to the advertisement but almost immediately the police were on our tail saying that the law forbade a 14-year-old to own a gun. We had imagined that on our own private property this did not apply. Apparently this was not the case, and Ben had to wait until his sixteenth birthday before he came by his gun and could go out and get me 'a couple for the pot'.

A few years later there was a strange sequel to this episode. In Guernsey there is a law called the Armes de Chasse law which forbids anyone to go on anyone else's land carrying a gun. It is a criminal offence to do so. However it became known in Guernsey that this law had never been applied to Herm. In the past anyone wishing to shoot rabbits in Herm had always approached Peter and sought permission, which he had almost invariably given— now, however, the situation suddenly became alarmingly different. At any time of the day or night we would be invaded by—quite literally—hordes of 'sportsmen'—and, since there was no law to gainsay them, their numbers even included young lads who were too young to hold a licence. The situation was impossible and none of us felt safe to leave our homes and gardens. More than one person was peppered by shot as he walked home up the hill—and we lost at least two valuable heifers, which, frightened by the noise of gunfire, bolted into barbed wire fences. Peter went to the Board of Administration and before many months were out the Armes de Chasse law was applied to Herm and peace reigned again. We came to an agreement with a recognised organisation of Guernsey rabbit shooters permitting them to come and shoot at specified times and this has worked amicably and satisfactorily and is no small aid in helping us to keep our rabbit population within reasonable bounds. This involves removing some 6,000 rabbits a year and we ourselves spend about £75 a year on cartridges alone.

In spite of this rigorous shooting policy some of the rabbits have become very tame, especially around the hotel area, and some slight consolation to our problem is to watch the delight children staying in the hotel get from watching them as they hop about on the hotel lawn. We have seen children creep up to a rabbit on all fours and actually stroke it before it hopped away, and cameras are constantly busy getting close-up shots of them. I often reflect ruefully what a pity it is that rabbits are such engaging creatures to look at; it is difficult to arouse public sympathy in a war against Flopsy Bunny with his nursery-book appeal.

Indeed, we are not proof against the sentimental approach ourselves and I remember on one occasion we were walking round the north end with Sapper when a rabbit emerged from a burrow almost at our feet. Sapper set off in pursuit and the bewildered rabbit turning first this way and then that ended up by rushing into the sea, whereupon Peter, with no hesitation at all, dashed into the sea after it and rescued the poor bedraggled creature and restored it safely to its burrow.

One small sideline which our rabbit population furnishes us with is the unlikely one of export of fleas. We have never had myxomatosis in Herm, and so our rabbit fleas are much sought after by a laboratory in Oxford where experiments are carried out in relation to the transmission of myxomatosis. For this it is important to have fleas from myxomatosis-free rabbits and so two or three times a year we send a consignment of fleas in polythene bags, with a supply of rabbit ears to keep them going, off to Oxford.

Nevertheless, despite these factors we do have a problem which in the interests of good husbandry would be best answered by a rigorous trapping policy.

There are from 150 to 200 pheasants on the island, depending on how good a breeding season it has been, and although they are a considerable nuisance in the garden, pecking at the tender new sprouts and peas, we like to see them around the island.

Occasionally we have shooting parties over and I remember after fixing up one such occasion by correspondence with a naval commander who was expecting to visit the island, as the result of a typographical error on my part, Peter received a letter from him saying that he was intrigued to see that we apparently led a fine feudal life on the island and that he would respect our wishes and "shoot as many rabbits as he liked but limit his bag to two or three peasants only"!

35

Upheaval Again

It was our habit, when visiting the children at their boarding schools during the summer term, to stay in a caravan park in Dorset, conveniently situated near their schools. The children much preferred the free and easy routine we led there to staying in an hotel, and it made a pleasant break for Peter and me too. It was there that we met Lou. He ran a small general stores in the corner of the park and we were impressed with his energy and drive and the way he set out his shop. We got to know him well over the various fortnights we spent there and when it came to looking for someone to manage the three new shops that the Italians had built for us, we thought of Lou and wrote to him. He flew over to look around, liked what he saw and decided to take the job offered him. We were not mistaken in our assessment of Lou, and over the years his drive and initiative has given the little shops all the colour and excitement of an Eastern bazaar, so that many a camera is levelled at their gay windows, filled with silk scarves from Italy and perfumes from France, while outside stalls are piled high with brightly-coloured hats and beach baskets. Annually the business which they did improved.

Still one thing remained of serious concern to us. For some while it had been becoming obvious that our public services were not adequate to the demands being put upon them, chief among these being our sewerage disposal system and also our sources of water supply. With our increased visitor population, both resident and, more particularly, daily, the water consumption had risen enormously. Crisis seemed to be the order of each day in high summer. We approached the Board of Administration again, and as ever, they were helpful. A loan was made to our public services department to enable us to put these things right, the loan was to be repaid annually as a first charge against the Poll Tax. In the winter of 1967-8 this work was put in hand. The improvement to the water supply, besides the enlarging of two of our existing wells, involved the putting in of float switches at each of the two reservoirs, so that they refilled completely automatically. Up until that time a man had had to go around daily and assess how much water was needed to fill them and how long the pump must run to do so, which was very absorbing of labour, and therefore costly to maintain. Peter welcomed this automation eagerly and for him it highlighted almost more than anything else up to then how far we had come since that first summer on the island when we had actually been shipping water over in drums from Guernsey.

This work on the water system had not been particularly disruptive to put in hand, but the sewage disposal system was another matter. It meant a tremendous amount of upheaval.

It seemed rather horrifying to disturb the little village area around the harbour which we had worked so hard to make beautiful, but we tried to project our minds forward to when it would all be straight again. The winter was a wet stormy one, and once the work started it was not long before we were picking our way through a sea of mud and upturned rubble, while the mechanical digger and men with spades and shovels ravaged the green hillside from the farm building down to the harbour, and dug trenches and laid pipes right through the village. I was glad that none of our summer visitors were there to see the mess and disorder, and wondered frantically if it would ever look trim and straight again, but Peter was reassuring, and so relieved was he to know that we were at last going to be efficiently served by water and the sewage system that the interim mess worried him far less than it did me. It was a scramble to get the work finished by the spring, but finished it was, and once the last pipe was in place we set about restoring the appearance of the village.

191

Over the last few years with this sort of thing in mind, we had asked John to make a nursery garden in part of the walled garden, and he had taken cuttings of many shrubs, including hydrangeas, fuchsias and veronicas, and now we planted some of these out and they quickly hid the scarred ground, so that in a few weeks it was impossible to tell what a ravaging had taken place.

With the island businesses now poised, as we hoped, to take full advantage of such trade as came our way, we felt we could legitimately turn our attention once again to our own home.

I imagine most people given the choice would elect to embark on a building project during the spring and summer months when some degree of certainty of good weather can be expected, but with us, once again it had to be the beginning of October when we set about extensive and, we hope, final alterations to our house and garden. We hoped to be able to do the work with labour drawn entirely from the island community and were very pleased when we found it possible to do this, the only exceptions being Jimmie and Paul, who, although both living in Guernsey now, came across to give us a helping hand and whom, anyway, we always regard as Herm Islanders.

We now had a new problem in relation to our home. Whereas in the past we seemed to have frequently recurring need for expansion as our family increased, now the reverse was the case, in fact what we now needed was the seemingly impossible, an elastic house which could expand when the holidays were upon us and all the children returned, frequently with friends, and contract during term time when Peter and I were on our own and had no desire to rattle around in a large and empty house. Moreover, as far as I was concerned I could do without the burden of keeping it all cleaned. Surprisingly enough we worked out a very liveable house, which, as it is on sloping ground, is two floors on one side and three on the other. It involved converting the house into a three-storey one—utilising to good effect the large area under the main floor of the house by the construction of a flight of stairs down to it. Somewhat to our surprise, we there contrived to achieve three bedrooms and bathroom, a trunk-room and a laundry-room. On the top floor we already had two double bedrooms, so that altogether we could easily accommodate all the children with room to spare for visiting friends. Both these two floors could be shut off when the children were away. This left the ground floor for living space and a bedroom for Peter and me. We practically gutted the wing of small bedrooms that we had built for the children some fourteen years previously and converted it into one large bedroom for ourselves with dressing-room and bathroom. It was not a difficult conversion and has proved to be a very pleasant one. We have given the room French windows which open straight on to the garden so that we can wake in the morning and look out across the garden to the fields beyond and see the cows grazing. We now had a large room to spare on the ground floor, one which had previously been our bedroom, to convert into a much needed larger drawing-room. So in a sense we had come full circle and arrived back where we had begun, and the room we had first entered twenty years ago and had had such a pleasant surprise when we saw its unexpectedly large and elegant proportions became a drawing-room again.

We were in a state of considerable upheaval for at least six months, the more so as we decided to give the garden a new look at the same time and this involved moving in a large mechanical digger. As before, it was brought across on the barge, this time behind the *Henry Rose*, at high tide so that it could be driven off on to the slipway at the harbour. Arrived at the garden it produced a scene of devastation and upset in no time at all, so that I at least could hardly bear to watch and had to hang on determinedly to the vision we had pictured of what it would be like in say a year's time. In fact it was less than that, much less. By the following Easter order was restored and we were hard at work replanting out the borders and sowing the lawn and, joy of joys, we had a fine new swimming pool to repay us

193

for our winter of mess and discomfort. We built a semi-circular sheltering wall around the pool below the level of the existing garden; this in no way impeded our view out across the garden to the sea and Guernsey.

The pool has given us all a lot of pleasure, not least the island children. They seem to learn to swim much faster in a pool than in the sea, which is a relief to parents as swimability is a very desirable acquisition here at as early an age as possible.

36

Sea Harvest

We all become very weather conscious, living on Herm. In England it sustains the conversation and dictates the wardrobe, but on Herm the weather controls the whole course of our daily lives. And what weather! As I write this mid-October and look out from my window overlooking the wide sea, it could just as easily be mid-May. The sun is just as warm, the sea as blue, and only the golden-brown shades of the bracken on Monku gives a clue to the season—and yet a week ago, when I had planned to go to Guernsey for the day, I woke to find lowering clouds and a fresh wind whipping the wave tops into blown spume—making it expedient to consult the skipper of the boat as to when would be the best time to make the crossing, when would the wind and tide combine to make the sea least rough, or would it be prudent not to go at all? Never does the phrase, "Man proposes, but God disposes", seem more evident than on occasions like these.

Even in summer the weather can be capricious, and we may have several days at a stretch when the only boat to venture across is our own *Henry Rose*, to pick up the milk, and the visitors from Guernsey do not come over; but generally it is sunshine, blue skies and a light warm wind blowing from the south-west.

Spring is wonderful. Our focus changes from the sea to the burgeoning trees and the grass. Spring comes early to Herm. In fact, I see from my diary that during the third week in January for the last three years, I have picked a small bunch of primroses. From then on they appear with greater frequency until by mid-March the hillsides are pale yellow with them, and the copses white with blackthorn interspersed with the brilliant gold of gorse.

Winter is perhaps my favourite time of all—especially when the weather closes in and heightens our sense of island isolation. People frequently say to me, "Herm must be lovely in the summer, but what on earth do you do in the winter?"

My answer is, "Well much the same as you do I suppose," although upon reflection, I imagine this is not really true. For me, although not beleaguered by the weather and the fact that we have but one boat in and out of the island daily, my boundaries are set, and life is centred upon my home to a greater extent than if I lived in England. I am never further than fifteen minutes' walk away from it, and yet by walking round the coast I can walk for an hour and a half, a fact which surprises people when they consider that the island is only 1½ miles by ½ mile.

Beachcombing sometimes plays a diverting part in our autumn and winter lives. I can think back to the dramatic episode of the *Flying Enterprise*, which after a tremendous storm lay with a very heavy list off Land's End for several days before finally sinking. Some days later dozens of mailbags were washed up on the north beaches. We dried them out as best we could and then handed them over to the Receiver of Wreck in Guernsey. The beaches were also littered with thousands of wax candles, most of them still in perfect condition. There is a limit to the number of candles any household can find useful, but I imagine we were better qualified than most to avail ourselves of the unexpected harvest, served as we were then by oil lamps and an erratic electrical supply. Then there was the cargo of pit props which came ashore on our north-west beaches, washed off the decks of a timber ship from Scandinavia during a storm. Many of these proved enormously useful, and were incorporated to good effect in alterations we had in hand at the time in the Mermaid. We still have some in store and frequently have recourse to them in building projects.

From my point of view perhaps the most exciting haul of all came in the winter of 1970, when a cargo of Seville oranges was washed ashore in Belvoir bay and along the length of Shell Beach. Only that week I had spoken to my greengrocer in Guernsey asking him to let me know as soon as the Seville oranges were in, as I was anxious to make a start with marmalade making. Harvest of the seas indeed! Whole crates were carried into the island homes and womenfolk got busy over their preserving pans, anxious to get the fruit used before the salt action of the seawater seeped into the skins and spoilt the fruit. By a coincidence, earlier that week I had bought a magazine and one of the pages was devoted exclusively to recipes using oranges. I tried them all and very good most of them were. By the end of a couple of weeks I had 98 pounds of marmalade and about 20 pounds of orange curd. Needless to say I soon ran out of jars to put it all in, so Peter on his way home from the office every day would make a detour round the south end to an old rubbish dump which hadn't been used since before the war and there he dug around and came home each time laden down with an assortment of old jars of all shapes and sizes, and we soon had them all filled.

One rather amusing aspect of this orange bonanza was that in the weeks that followed, there wasn't a duck to be bought in Guernsey, where crates had also been washed up, as obviously everyone was trying out their various duck à l'orange recipes!

Another unlikely find was when clambering among the rocks on the east coast between Belvoir and the south end one winter's afternoon, we came across a number of shattered packing cases, and lodged in the crevices between the rocks all manner of Revlon cosmetics, nail varnishes, hair lacquer, lipsticks galore! The word flew round and the women of the island had another field day.

The winter weather can be tough and boisterous, cold even, but even in midwinter we can be surprised by a mild spell, when it is possible to take a picnic lunch to one of the beaches.

The work goes on, although at a more measured pace, there is always maintenance of the buildings to be done, possibly the planning and building of some new development and as the turn of the year comes, painting and decorating to get ready for the season ahead.

Life on Herm divides itself quite sharply into two halves. After six months of having the island entirely to ourselves, with the coming of spring we find ourselves looking forward to seeing fresh faces about, the movement of boats on the sea and a speed-up in the tempo of living. The summer seasonal staff come flooding back into the island and our resident population leaps from about forty to a hundred almost overnight. The little shops come alive and are gay with merchandise, the beach cafés open up their shutters and hang beach balls and buckets and spades outside their windows and the hotel, so still and silent through the winter months, once again reverberates to chatter and laughter and pulses with life.

Everyone has to be versatile, and we have no room for the unionist who cannot be called upon at a moment's notice to help out on a job, probably quite different from the one which he was engaged to perform—so that a man who came to help in the office may well find himself hard at it cutting sandwiches in a beach café during a peak period of activity. We spend our summertime among people who are relaxed and happy and on holiday so that we tend to see only the nicest side of people, who have time to talk and be friendly, and in these days of constant outside pressures, this is surely a rare state of affairs. We like these two contrasting halves to the year which prevent life ever becoming dull or monotonous.

Nevertheless, life on Herm, so satisfying to Peter and me, has not always proved to be everyone's cup of tea. Some have come to us—many with a genuine desire to make a success of it—only to find after a matter of a few months that island life was not for them; they missed having numerous social contacts, the cinema and theatre, and ability to pop to the shops on a moment's impulse, and

198

have found it exasperating when a planned trip to Guernsey has had to be suddenly scrapped because the sea has been too rough. Such people quickly return whence they came. Apart from these birds of passage there are others who stay with us for four or five years and then move on. We think the reason is that the very thing that brings them to us in the first place, call it a pioneering spirit or what you will, is the very same driving force that persuades them after an interval of time to move on again. We understand this, inconvenient from our point of view though it may be.

Mick and Bunty have fallen into this category and have now moved over to Guernsey, where they have developed their own small but thriving business; and Pat and George left us many years ago to run their own hotel in Sark. But their places have been taken by others, Wendy and Derek and their children; and Joan and Dennis, Bryan and Judith and their family of four young children; and Dick and Joan and their two boys, and these have joined the hardy nucleus of staunch people like Phil and Nina and John and Mary who have been with us from the beginning and who have become deeply identified with Peter and me and all we strive for.

Last year we built a modern, up-to-date schoolroom. It has been converted from an old farm building at the top of the hill and it adjoins the home of the schoolmistress, Joan and her husband Dick. Her own two boys attend the school and, because by design the schoolroom opens out from her kitchen, she can easily combine the rôles of school teacher and housewife. This school succeeds a room we had been using in one of the farm cottages and which, as our community grew, had become inadequate to our needs. Looking around the light, airy classroom with its bright paintwork and gay linoleum on the floor, we seem in many respects to have come a long way from the schoolroom in the old keep where ivy pushed in at the ill-fitting windows and buckets were placed at strategic positions about the floor to catch the drips when it rained. Yet, as before, the sight and sound of the varied island activities is never very far away from the schoolroom. Work goes on to the accompaniment of the hum and throb of the electric generators which are housed in the barn across the yard where they play. A small boy's eyes may well be diverted to the enthralling spectacle of, possibly, his Dad at work on one of the tractors brought into the repair shop yard opposite for overhaul. Then the happy distraction as the afternoon wears on of watching, and maybe counting, the slow procession of the milking herd of some sixty or more cows as they meander down the lane and past the school windows for milking.

There are altogether twelve families living on the island now. Sometimes when Peter and I look around at their homes, well furnished and equipped, cosy and comfortable, we think back to the time when we stood in the chapel on that first visit to Herm and tried to think what precisely our life would be like were we to take Mr. Jefferies's offer when he said, "If you like the place you can have it. It's on the market."

I remember also that when we rushed back to England, our minds made up and concerned lest someone had beaten us to it, Mr. Jefferies said that he had indeed had offers and expected more which possibly would better ours, but at once he accepted us with the words, "I want you two to have it."

I don't think we had the slightest idea what was in store for us, but this I know—had we then in a moment of foresight been able to see, as, looking back we can now, what troubles and problems lay ahead of us and how hard won each achievement was to be we might indeed have been daunted, but we would still have gone on. Fortunately, knowledge of the future is denied one, but the view that we then did have very clearly, of Herm being a living place, of families, of a school, the church, all of us living by our united efforts out of the natural resources of the island *has* become a reality. Where, when we came to Herm, there was dereliction; now there is the pulse of life. Houses are homes again, children are born here, Mum is the centre of her home. A home where Dad is not a shadowy figure 'at

200

the office' but is known to be nearby doing something which can not only be seen, but be seen to be necessary to the life of the community.

We have been here for over twenty-three years now and, setting aside something big and terrible happening, I think that we, and ours, will stay here for ever. There is to me something strange and compelling in the thought that Peter and I have breathed new life into this lovely little plot, where a people's history has spanned so many centuries and which is discernible in the prehistoric graves of Neolithic man, in the massive monastic walls that enclose the fields, in the church and houses whose very alterations speak of the passage of a thousand years.

Our problems are many and deeply concern us, but we live a life of endeavour and a measure of success has come our way, not only in the business but in the kind of life we lead.

The island children have, I think, a rather special kind of background; as to whether it will help or hinder them in their lives I do not know, but certainly they will never forget it. Perhaps one or two of them will come back to put their backs into the job and will continue where—and when—Peter and I leave off.

Four of our own children have left school now and are out in the world learning their chosen professions, and two are still at school in England.

Herm is very dear to all of them and coming home means more than just to our house and garden. Home is undoubtedly Herm, where every island path and hill and field, every little bay, almost every rock along the coast has been known to them since early childhood.

Certainly I think that all the children of the island will, as we parents do in our various ways, put some special value on living here where our work is closely related to our living, where there is bird-song to listen to, where the sun sinks into a clear sea, and where, even during a busy day, one can now and again stop and be deeply content with the sight and scent of the countryside, the clean tang of the sea and take time in fact, once in a while, simply to stand and stare.

Lady Perry's House   *Herm Island 1971*

The Years that Followed

So that is Peter's and my story. Or almost so. I have always felt that even though many years have elapsed since 'Herm our Island Home' was published the story was a complete one and that to add to it might well detract rather than embellish. How can the events of more recent times possibly have the nostalgic appeal of those early days? Nostalgia is a strange thing and seems to take no account of past difficulties, uncertainty and worry. How can it be that I look back on those first twenty or so years with wistful memories when things are so much better now? So I had decided to 'leave it at that' in spite of the question sometimes asked me by people who ask 'what about the next bit? when are you going to tell us about what happened afterwards?', but a remark recently made to Peter by a German travel writer persuaded me that perhaps there was more that should be told and which would be of interest.

As they walked up the hill to the church and to our house, Peter, who had been extolling the many virtues of Herm as a holiday venue, paused to point out the very fine cast iron lamp standard with copper lamp which the islanders had presented to us to commemorate our having lived in Herm for a third of a century. "Do you mean to say that you have lived here for thirty-three years?"

"Well more, as a matter of fact, it's now thirty-six years" Peter replied.

"But that is incredible" said the German. "Thirty-six years, a lifetime's work, in the same place; In this day and age don't you realise how unusual that is, and you're still at it. Now that *is* a story."

37

Family Matters

Familywise a lot of water has passed under the bridge in the last fifteen years. Five of our children, as well as Margaret, are now married and two of them, Ben and Jo, live with their families in New Zealand, which is sad in that they are so far away and we see little of them, but as Peter is himself a New Zealander it is, I suppose, not surprising. At least it gives Peter and me a good reason for taking a trip 'down under' every now and again to visit them and to catch up on our new grandchildren as they arrive. Indeed as I write we are sailing down the Panama Canal on just such a trip. It's interesting but very humid and hot and we look forward to arriving in Auckland and the cooling breezes of the Land of the Long White Cloud.

Ben with his wife Jan, who he met amd married in New Zealand in 1978, are fruit growing, mainly Kiwifruit, in the Northland of New Zealand. They have four children, Kate, Guy, Hamish and Juliet.

Jo is married to David, a Jerseyman, and together they emigrated to New Zealand five years ago. They have two small schoolboy sons, Sam and Oliver, and David recently graduated with a degree in agriculture from Massey University and is now with ICI in Auckland.

Margaret is also still distanced from us as she and Tim, her husband, run a summer camp and environmental education centre in Maine on a lovely pineclad stretch of the New England coastline. Several of her Herm 'brothers and sisters' have been to stay with her to see their nephew and niece, Ben and Jenny, growing up and to help as counselors for the three month summer season. But Simon and Helen his wife, a Yorkshire girl, and their three children Matthew, Sophie and Adam live nearer to hand in Guernsey so we see them frequently and Herm is still very much a part of their lives. As it is also with Rupert who married Sharon, another Yorkshire girl, in our own Island church, St. Tugal's, on a golden June day in 1984. This was a lovely family reunion in which we were once again all together for the first time in fifteen years, Ben and Jo from New Zealand, Margaret from America. Rupert and Sharon now have a little son, Alec.

Pennie and Rosemary live even closer for they are in Herm. However Rosemary is to be married this summer to Rupert, a Guernseyman, — another Rupert in the family! — and another occasion for a family reunion and a wedding in our own church and garden. Pennie and her husband Adrian, who took over as Island manager from Simon, when he went to live in Guernsey in 1980, live in the Manor House which stands four square across a sweep of lawn beside the church, an elegant and dignified transition from the dilapidated shell we found when we first saw it well over a third of a century ago. Hannah and Zoë, their two small daughters attend the same little island school where Pennie herself made her first wobbly letters and mastered the sentences in her 'Janet and John' book. Two of our twelve grandchildren, Ben and Jan's little son Guy and Zoë, Adrian and Pennie's daughter, arrived within an hour of each other, one in each hemisphere!

Woolly Bear has left the island to live in honourable retirement in Guernsey, and so has Pandora, but in their place is Katie, a spotted grey and white donkey, as much beloved by Hannah and Zoë as was her predecessor by their mother. She shares her paddock with other well loved friends, Petal and Fleur, two Golden Guernsey goats. Katie has a brightly coloured little cart in which, occasionally, Pennie drives the children, but mostly Hannah and Zoë ride bareback. A more recent arrival and very much a newcomer to the Island is Pennie's horse, a well mannered and friendly animal called Bianco. A strange name for a bay with a black mane, but perhaps his one white foot justifies it. Because of the stony outcrops around the island Pennie decided that the children must wear riding hats and accordingly went to Guernsey to get them, where she found that all she could get in a size that would fit was the helmet type hard hat worn by young BMX riders. Zoë took one look at this enormous contraption and flatly refused to wear hers. Pennie cajoled and reasoned and eventually resorted to a straight command, 'Put it on at once' she said and Zoë, muttering darkly 'Alright, but I'll prob'ly die' obeyed. Hannah was more compliant and put hers on without demur, but Pennie and I looking on caught each others' eye and almost burst out laughing; she looked exactly like a tadpole with her outsized black head and slim little body. We managed to control our mirth for had she had the slightest inkling how comical she looked she would without doubt have refused to wear hers too.

Mimosa has joined Sapper in, we like to think, other equally happy, although celestial fields, and in their place are Teazle, Pennie's dog and Twiggy, Peter's and mine; Yorkshire terriers both. Scanning the 12" survey map of Herm, which Peter updates from time to time, you would see that they each share what is, I imagine, an unusual if not unique canine distinction, namely a feature named after them. The Teazle, a furzy copse in the middle of the North Common and Twiggy Wood, a hitherto unnamed spinney beside the Drive. Bramble, Adrian's dog, a springer spaniel has achieved a distinction of another kind. Her effigy forms the weather vane fixed to a gable end on one of the old farm buildings in Le Manoir. Pennie drew her outline on a sheet of copper which Adrian produced by flattening out a burst water cylinder. He then cut it out and mounted it on a fine bronze N.S.E. & W. which he unearthed in one of the barns. There must be something amiss with the balance however, because sometimes she displays elements of indecision and vagaries of temperament that she never displays in real life. One moment she is assuring us that the wind is due west, the next, changing her mind and swinging hesitantly to the south, and then she performs a sudden flick round almost the entire compass as though to say 'Oh no, I'm sorry, I mean East!' However, its a very handsome vane and for the most part she gets the direction right. In any case we have come to regard the flag which, except in gale conditions, flutters from the flag pole on the keep, as the most reliable indicator of wind direction.

38

The March of Progress

On the island itself, though much has changed much remains the same so that landing on the harbour on any June morning as we did some thirty seven years ago you would still hear the oyster catchers piping, see the terns circling over Hermetier and as you turned inland and climbed the hill towards Le Manoir catch the elusive scent of honeysuckle, the warm coconut smell of gorse and, by the meadow of Valley Panto, the pungent drift of eucalyptus and pine. These things will never change nor that almost tangible quality of peace and tranquility that laps around you as soon as you set foot in Herm, so that it would still be true to say as Sir Philip Neame, the then Governor of Guernsey said when he first came to Herm in 1948 'This is the nearest approach to Fairyland that I have ever seen or will ever hope to see'. Not the first of these kind of comments—Lady Dorothy Osbourne, in a love letter written in 1653 recalled her magical childhood yearning for Herm: 'Do you remember Arme and the little house there? Shall we go thither? That's next to being out of the world. There we might live together like Baucis and Philemon, grow old together in our little cottage and for our charity to some shipwrecked strangers obtain the blessing of dying both at the same time.'

Of the various enterprises on the island it is doubtful whether returning visitors are at first conscious of any great change, indeed we hope that they are not, but Peter and I are. For instance we now have a fine new Power House, housing three 64KW deisel powered generators. Our old single phase generators which we installed in the mid 60's were reaching the end of their useful lives and inevitably needing a lot of maintenance. With a certain amount of 'open heart surgery' from time to time they finally limped home in 1984. These new plants are water cooled and are much quieter as they smoothly and comparatively silently go about their job keeping the island going.

The shipping over and installation of the new generators was one of the most interesting and involved tasks we had had up to that date and required, as all unusual shipments of expensive machinery do, special marine insurance over and above our normal policy. Timing was of the essence and first of all the Power House had to be got ready to receive them. It had to be upgraded to a standard befiting such fine new equipment. Better ventilation was required, the inside walls must be stripped of old pipes and shelves which had long since become obsolete, but which still draped the walls; a sturdier floor must be laid to take the generators themselves, and lastly the whole building had to be steam cleaned and decorated. Then came the job of getting the new generators across from Guernsey where they had arrived from England. Each generator weighed in at one and a half tons approximately, and there was also a large instrument panel which weighed one ton and so it all had to come across in two loads.

From the moment it was planned Adrian's greatest concern in master minding the operation was the weather, as it always is when shipping is involved. On this occasion fortune certainly smiled upon us for over the crucial period the sea maintained an almost glassy calm.

Over in Guernsey a lorry was craned onto the deck of the Trident and onto the lorry were craned two of the three generators. At the Herm end the Trident was secured stern on to the harbour and when the tide was exactly right the lorry was driven off and up the hill to the area outside the Power House by the tractor barn. A JCB excavator, which we had on the island on other work and which was still there, was used to lift the generators, very gingerly, off the back of the lorry and to transport them onto rollers outside the Power House doors.

Then all that was needed was a lot of island man power and, inevitably, a lot of advice from the women and children who had gathered to watch the operation.

The following day the lorry was sent back to Guernsey and the whole process repeated for the remaining generator and the instrument panel. Their installation complete, next came the job of switching over from the old generators to the new. To maintain essential services throughout the operation one of the old generators had to remain in service until two of the new ones were ready to take over, so for a while we had a much depleted source of power and all of us had to get used to using very little electricity while the transfer was in progress. Woe betide any of us who unthinkingly switched on even an electric iron! Candles were always at the ready during this period as blackouts were not too unusual, putting Peter and me in mind of early days on the island. When the installation was nearing completion we decided to have a ceremonial 'opening' of our new Power House to celebrate what was to us another milestone in our island history. Accordingly we sent out a number of invitations to members of the Board of Administration in Guernsey and invited the wife of the President of the Board to 'switch on'. The Press and TV were also invited. There was to be a Vin d'Honneur following the switch on. We studied the tide table, a first requirement in planning any operation involving the boat, and fixed the date, two dates in fact, in case the first one should be ruled out because of adverse weather conditions. The invitations were sent out and in the most part accepted. Then the clerk of the weather stepped in and took a hand. To say that it was rough is to put it mildly. We entered into such a period of rain and storm as none of us could remember for years. Not only was the first date 'scrubbed' but the second one as well, so our generators slid quietly into their first 'chug chug' unheralded and unsung. The Power House is, however, a delight to see, clean and white, every polishable part of the engines on their red tile floor shining and bright so that even the least mechanically

210

minded of us take pride in taking our visiting friends to see it.

The menfolk on the island always seem to have an extra-sensory ability to detect any variation in the normally smooth sounding note from the engines. I have sometimes seen Peter, who I imagined to be deep in a book, get up from his chair and move towards the Power House saying 'That engine noise doesn't sound right', only to find that either Michael or Adrian or both are there before him, checking and adjusting. This was once a fairly common occurrence, but seldom happens now.

On a small island like this it is brought home very clearly how much one depends on the smooth running of the Power House and an unfailing supply of electricity. Cows are milked, refrigerators run, water pumped and sewage disposed of, to say nothing of house lighting and radio telephone. Looking back to the excitement we felt when our first 17 line telephone exchange was installed and we first made contact with the world outside our small island, little did we imagine that the day would come when we would have 84 lines, with full STD world wide capability; Looking back still further to the days when we had no telephone at all! So, setting expense aside for the moment (although regrettably it is a factor to be considered, therefore it is a pleasure normally reserved for birthdays and Christmas), it is a matter of no difficulty whatsoever to pick up the 'phone, tap out a somewhat lengthy number and within seconds be speaking to either Ben or Jo and their families in New Zealand or to Margaret in America. Their voices as clearly to be heard as if they were in the next room.

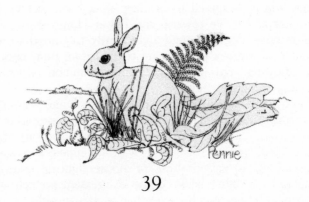

39

We improve our water supply

Our present water supply is another source of considerable satisfaction, and indeed, amazement to us. We can remember all too well summers when we had to ask everyone, guests as well as islanders to be sparing with the use of water and in fact we actually had to resort to shipping over drinking water from Guernsey in milk churns during that first drought summer when we first arrived on the island. For many years we used sea water to flush all WCs. Under drought conditions we may still ask for reasonable care in seeing that water is not wasted but this is now rarely necessary.

Two years ago a dream became reality when we installed, not without trial and tribulation, a fresh water swimming pool at the north end of the long lawn to the south of the hotel. No sooner was the hole dug than the heavens opened and work had to cease for several weeks while the pool slowly filled with muddy water and we gazed dispiritedly at it and tried to imagine the finished product. But the weather did eventually clear up, the pool was pumped out, work went frantically ahead and was at last completed, and I'm sure that guests arriving that spring could not have visualised just how desolate it had all looked a few weeks earlier. Peter landscaped the pool into the surrounding terrain so that it has different levels of lawn around it and the rising hill behind it to the east provides a necessary shelter from any wind in that quarter. An old Spanish chestnut tree, whose fate at one stage, when the digging started, hung in the balance, was reprieved and is now seen to add enormously to the established look that the pool quickly achieved.

Testimony also to our much improved and increased water supply which follows on drilling more deep bore holes, is that we can look back to a time when even to be able to water our lawn was merely a pipe dream of Peter's, a thing he quite literally dreamt about, but now, *mirabile dictu*, not only can we water our lawn, but can look across our garden over the paddock where Katie and the goats graze to the Home Field beyond, and see on any hot dry summer's day a myriad water jets spraying across the grass, 10,000 gallons a day, irrigating in turn, either that field or, just across the Spine Road, Big Seagull Field.

40

The Island Boats Today

Our improved electrical supply has also made possible very necessary navigational leading lights to both the harbour and the Rosaire landing. It is, I suppose in this latter respect, communication with Guernsey by boat, where the most outward and obvious sign of change and development lie. It is hard to remember now just how rugged and uncomfortable sea travel in the *Arrowhead* or even the *Henry Rose* could be when a strong wind of anything more than a force 4 or 5 prevailed, which it frequently does in winter months. But gone are those days now; gone also the anxious peering out to sea trying to pick out the small boat from among the turbulent white capped waves, for the *Trident* arrives with precision like punctuality so that you could 'set your watch' by her regular arrivals and departures. The *Trident* belongs to the Trident Charter Company run by Charlie, a familiar figure to all who come this way and an old friend of ours. Some years ago he and Simon put their heads together and came up with a chartering proposition. The outcome was that we sold the *Henry Rose*, thus relieving ourselves of all the problems of administering and running our own boat service. It had always represented one of our chief trouble areas, consuming a lot of time and energy which we could ill afford, so this charter arrangement had the immediate attraction of leaving us free to concentrate our efforts on other island activities and administration. Under the agreement the Trident Charter Company are obligated to meet all of our passenger and cargo shipping needs and this they do extremely well to our mutual advantage. It suits us well and, we have no doubt, it suits them well too as they now have an all the year round revenue coming in from us, so I suppose you could say that the arrangement is mutually supportive, a kind of symbiotic relationship.

Travelling aboard the *Trident* en route to Guernsey, Peter and I often reflect on the quite incredible advance from those early days. To begin with boarding the boat, no scrambling over a possibly heaving gunwhale onto a seat and then to slatted deck timbers below; the *Trident* is a large power driven catamaran and now one steps serenely onto a flat deck which is level with the harbour and then into the passenger deck where one sits in an individual comfortable seat. On the *Arrowhead* we had just a compass; on the *Trident* there is radar, ship to shore radio and, surely the ultimate in sophistication, fitted carpet throughout! The boat can be covered or open as the weather dictates. For cargo carrying it is excellent, bringing in all our day to day supplies, cattle feed and fertilisers in 10 ton lots and daily up to 200 gallons of milk out and over to Guernsey. From time to time when we need it, it will bring over a special load — such as a 9 ton JCB excavator, and recently it ferried across to us a 14 ton borehole drilling rig with no great difficulty, which in the old days would have been quite a problem to get across.

As for the children's rowing and sail boats of earlier days, these have mostly given way to sail boards and to larger outboard engined Dorys, the latter being very convenient for a quick trip to Guernsey for Adrian and his family or a quick trip to Herm for Simon or Rupert and their families; or, perhaps, for a lazy hour or two in the blue sand fringed lagoons to the North of the island.

Board sailing is now a very popular pastime in these waters, a wonderfully exhilarating challenge to skill and agility as they skim over the sea at the speed of the wind like brightly coloured butterflies.

215

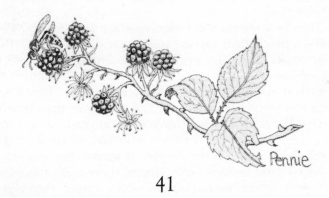

Pennie

41

Growth — Hotels and Farming

In these intervening years we felt we could and should expand and during this period we added two hotels and a restaurant and public house business in Guernsey. This was a busy time for Peter involving many comings and goings and much time spent away from the island, a necessary time, we felt, but not one that either he or I look back upon with any great degree of pleasure, although it was interesting. But in the event it was, we feel, a right and proper thing to have done for after a few years, and when they were ready and equipped to do so, first Simon and then Rupert took over these enterprises from us, have put their own stamp upon them so are now set up in their own businesses and Peter and I continue in Herm, which is where it all started and where we want to be.

With Adrian, our son-in-law, Pennie's husband, as island manager taking the greater part of the load from his shoulders, Peter is now free to enjoy those aspects of island life which appeal to him the most. One of the things he is now able to do and enjoys is to spend more time walking about the island and over the farm where upwards of 120 sleek Guernseys now placidly graze or walk in gently plodding file to be milked in the new farm buildings which we constructed in Little Seagull field over 10 years ago. Another project which ran into early problems on account of the weather. We turned, I remember, the first sod at the beginning of what was to be one of the wettest winters we had ever had so that our plans and schemes foundered for week after week in a sea of squelchy mud and sodden grass. Ben was home at the time and he supervised tractor load after tractor load of shingle from the Oyster Rocks Beach for the concrete foundations which, once the land had sufficiently dried out, we laid for the 8 x 8 herring-bone milking parlour and dairy which stands there today, along with a 100 cow cubicle building and calf rearing and bull pens.

The farm has indeed come a long way since Peter and I turned into the farmyard, within a few hours only of our first ever landing on Herm to see six Guernseys being hand milked and to stroke the soft warm golden coats of the two little calves, which were to be the foundation stock of our present herd.

In our early negotiations with the States of Guernsey the experts told us that they considered that a profitable farm could never be run on Herm and as such 'we could forget all about it', there would be no obligation for us to farm the land. But we felt strongly that this was a wrong decision. Nor would we accept it. The concept of this lovely little island with the farm lands unkempt, rabbit infested, covered in bracken and bramble, as we had found them was a totally alien one to us. Also, without doubt the fact that our early dreams centred so much on the countryside and farming conditioned us to make a determined effort to succeed and not even to contemplate the possibility of failure. Setbacks there have certainly been, as for instance when in the early days we went in for pig breeding and set ourselves up with a breeding stock, sties and farrowing pens

217

and in the fullness of time were in production. A year later the subsidy on pork was removed and we found we could not compete with imported pork prices, so the venture came to an abrupt end. Another costly setback was an unusually serious infestation of leather-jackets, the larvae of Daddy-long-legs, affecting several of our best fields which we had just re-seeded with an expensive grass ley. We lost the lot, had to re-seed, and were without the necessary feed when it was wanted and with again the need to buy.

But the most dreadful day of all was yet to come. In 1976 we had to make the decision to slaughter 24 cows because of the year's drought which had turned our green island into a yellowish brown desert, and we hadn't enough to feed them on, short of expensive buying. In fact we did buy, in so far as we could afford to, and had bales of wheatstraw shipped to us from East Anglia, the nearest available source, for the drought was widespread and fodder in short supply everywhere.

This was at a time when we had set ourselves up to milk 100 from a total herd of about 130 and were working towards this. After this harrowing experience we realised that a more realistic target would be to milk 80 with an overall herd of 110, so once again circumstance and experience forced a sensible decision upon us, but it was a sad way to find out. These animals were ours, we knew them by name and many of them were descended from that first stock we had bought with Herm 25 years before, and to have firstly to decide to slaughter and then to choose which ones was poignant indeed.

So it has not been plain sailing by any means, but nevertheless the overall trend has been in an upward direction, and today the Herm farm although not large by English standards, is one of the bigger Guernsey farms. We supply Guernsey with 3% of its milk. But what is more important to us and a source of greater satisfaction is that it is periodically rated, in the way these things are assessed, as being at, or near, the top of the efficiency league.

42

Salvage

When we need building materials we usually ship them in from Guernsey although we are capable of making our own concrete blocks from shingle collected from the beach, and in the past for small scale building jobs we did this quite frequently, giving the blocks as rough a quality as possible to improve the texture of the finished work. We have also a lot of building granite on the island and whenever possible we build with this local material.

But sometimes, as in the case of the pitprops which drifted onto our shores many years ago, we have an unexpected windfall from the sea to help along our 'building and maintenance' programme.

A sad story lies behind one such happening. A large and ancient cargo ship *The Prosperity* sailing from Scandinavia to Greece in the winter of 1974 got into serious difficulties when a gale of exceptional hurricane force struck as they were off Guernsey. We remember the storm well, and it was the worst we have experienced here. The Master and First Mate were swept overboard when the whole deckhouse was washed away and the ship wrecked on the rocky west coast of Guernsey. The rest of the crew, young and inexperienced and without leadership took to the ship's boats and were almost immediately lost. All eighteen of them. Had they stayed with the ship which remained firmly wedged on the reef most, if not all, would probably have been saved.

The cargo consisted of very high quality timber designated for furniture manufacture and most of these magnificent

219

baulks were washed up all around the coast of Guernsey and a great number of them on our Herm beaches. Every man on the island was busily engaged for days in salvaging them and tractoring them up for storage in our barns. In due course the insurance assessors came over and put a price on them, and since this was considerably lower than we could have bought them for, we bought the lot.

We used a lot of the timber in the construction of the new farm, and we still have some of it,—'Prosperity timber' as we refer to it—in store for future use.

43

St. Tugual's Church

A year or two ago we put in hand some work on the church. The outside west wall had long ago been plastered over and Peter had decided to remove the plaster and expose the granite work, much of which must be Norman. When one is doing something like this and old stones come to light one longs for them to be able to speak. The decision was to have an unexpected reward. As the plasterer chipped away he discovered two blocked up windows high up, above and on either side of the west door. These little windows were in the thickness of the wall 3'6" and about 15" wide by 23" high. For some time we had been considering putting in another stained glass window over the door in the north transept, opposite and pairing with the one depicting Christ stilling the waves, in the south wall, given us by my father in 1966 and had decided that it should show Christ saying to the fishermen 'Follow me and I will make you Fishers of Men'. When we found these additional two small windows we both instantly felt that they should certainly not be blocked up again and that they too should be of stained glass. As to what their themes should be exercised our minds for some time and the rest of the family were called in to make suggestions. When taking the Sunday service Peter sometimes calls attention to the church building itself and tells of the way it was built by the Normans, a people who had a complete certainty of the existence of God in their lives, that He was always aware of what they thought and did and to whose voice they listened. So we all felt what could be better themes than stories of people who listened to God, and then did what God told them to do. Since the first window represented a New Testament story and so would its pair we decided that these two small windows should depict stories from the Old Testament. We went to Exeter and commissioned the same firm of stained glass makers who had made our first window to make these new ones. Needless to say the designs went backwards and forwards between Exeter and Herm for many weeks but finally came the day when Peter and I went again to Exeter to see the windows taking shape, just as Dad had done many years before, to see the first window being made.

If you stand in the church today and look up to the small west windows you will see that the one on the left is of the child Samuel in the temple being told by Eli to reply to the voice of God 'Speak Lord for thy servant heareth', and in the other window, Noah whom God instructed—'And God said unto Noah'—to build a boat and indeed, exactly how to build it, and who at once set about and built it. The window shows Noah standing by the Ark into which are filing two by two the animals. Nearest to the viewer are a Guernsey bull and cow, faithfully copied from photographs of two of our own animals. The window over the North door shows Christ standing as if on Herm harbour with the sweep of Fisherman's and Bears beaches, Monku and Petit Monceau hills and the islet of Hermetier in the background, — in the belief that Christ's command 'Follow Me' is as meaningful today in a modern setting as it was two thousand years ago on the shores of Galilee. In past years, more often than not we have been fortunate enough to have someone living on the island who could play our church organ, in fact before she married, and school terms when she was away excepted, Jo not invariably played for us at our Sunday service, but recently no-one living on the island has been able to do this. It occurred to Peter that if we were to install some sort of sound system with recorded hymns it would, in the absence of an organist, be a big help when it came to singing; so he arranged for a good local choir to

222

make us a tape recording of a selection of well known hymns.

Alas the idea, which had seemed to be such an excellent one, did not, in practice, work. It is hard to explain why, but somehow, singing to taped music without a conductor to bring the congregation in on cue is very difficult indeed. But since we had got the sound system Peter decided to leave it in the church although we do not use it during the service, so that anyone wanting to sit there at any time could listen to it, and this many of us do, and pleasant it is, especially on a summer evening with sunshine and birdsong outside, and inside, within those cool grey walls, quiet music playing.

In the garden by the west door there is now a life size figure of Christ. A convent in Guernsey was recently converted to other uses and Peter, hearing that this very old figure, probably of French origin was to lose its home asked if we might have it, so there it now stands, surrounded by trees and flowers, with calm dignified face and outstretched hand.

St. Tugual's Church has played an increasingly significant part in our family life. Three of our children have been married and all our children and grandchildren christened there.

pheasant

44

The Flagpole and Royalty

Many years ago, before the war in fact, walking on a south coast beach in England with a cousin who lived in the district, I found a carved wooden crown, about head size, wedged in a crevice of rock. It was a handsome thing, carved from solid wood and the faded paintwork was of red, gold and blue. Not knowing what its origin might be we took it to my Aunt's house and there it stayed for the next 40 years performing very effective service as a doorstop. A year or two ago, when both my cousin and her mother died and the contents of their home were being disposed of, someone, no doubt thinking of it as a useless artefact flung it to one side, where happily I saw it, perched on a pile of rubbish. Remembering having found it so long ago I took it and brought it back to Herm. It lay for several months in Peter's office-workshop—the one time 'guinea piggery'!—where one day John, the gardener, picked it up and said to Peter, "Do you know what this is?"

Peter replied, that no, he couldn't imagine what it could have been, so John told him that it was almost certainly the truck off the jack staff of a Royal Naval ship, which is always in the form of a crown. It was carved from oak and could be of any age, possibly even from the days of sailing men-of-war. Examining it more closely Peter saw the mortise for the masthead tenon and the recess for the halyard pulley block alongside.

Shortly after this discovery we put up a proper flagpole on Le Manoir Keep, which we had been intending to do for some time. Peter repainted the crown in its original bright heraldic colours and fixed it firmly to the top. So once again, after who knows how many years, it has come to perform a right and proper function.

We are not so isolationist on Herm, even in the winter months, as one might suppose and one of the things that has been a pleasure to us over the years have been the occasions when we have visited our lovely little neighbour island of Jethou. I remember one such occasion in 1974 when the then Crown Tenants of the Island, Sir Charles and Lady Hayward, invited us over to dine with them; short as the distance is between the islands a trip there can present problems of timing and tide, not to mention the possibility of a rough or splashy sea, so that the 'looking forward' is always tinged with a degree of concern. On this particular evening the weather was splashy to say the least and jumping ashore at Jethou on to the long landing ramp, where it runs down into the sea, Peter in a DJ, I in a long evening dress had an element of excitement, not unmixed with comedy; our fellow guests on that occasion were Sir Hugh and Lady Wontner. Sir Hugh and Lady Wontner were at that time the Lord Mayor and Lady Mayoress of London and as we sat in the lovely Manor House drawing room looking down across the narrow passage of water to Jethou's little offshore islet of Crevichon we talked of the masses of granite which had been quarried from it to build much of St. Peter Port harbour over one hundred and fifty years ago and then looking beyond Crevichon to Herm we told Sir Hugh that the steps which lead down from Waterloo Place to the Carlton House Terrace along the Mall in London were made from Herm granite, a fact which both surprised and interested him. When we came to leave we asked our hosts if we might steal their guests for the following day, and so it was that Sir Hugh and Lady Wontner were both in church that Sunday morning.

Before announcing the last hymn Peter asked the Island children if they all knew the story of Dick Whittington and his cat? Enthusiastic murmurs of 'yes!' and 'I do!' — so when Peter told them that in the congregation that morning there was a real live Lord Mayor of London, and that no doubt they would be able to talk to him and shake him by the hand afterwards, their wonder and delight was lovely to see, although the younger ones must have been a bit confused because at least two of them went home and related how they had been talking to Dick Whittington!

Although on several occasions in recent years, members of the Royal Family have visited the Bailiwick of Guernsey, so far we have not had the honour of a visit to Herm, and perhaps after a recent incident any aspirations we have in that direction may have suffered a setback. Last summer the Queen Mother visited Guernsey and Peter got out our extra specially big Union Jack to fly from the top of the Keep. "Can I put it up?" begged our granddaughter Sophie, who was staying with us at the time. Peter agreed so she and her friend, Georgina, rushed off and disappeared inside the Keep. Soon afterwards we saw the large flag fluttering at the masthead. It was only at sundown when Peter climbed up the tower himself to take it down that he realised with dismay that it had been flying upside down all day. *Lesé majesté* indeed!

Probably the last occasion upon which a member of the Royal family set foot on Herm was a visit made by one of Queen Victoria's granddaughters. This we discovered when later that same year we received an invitation from Sir Hugh Wontner bidding us to a private dinner party at The Mansion House. One of the other guests was the Princess

Alice, Countess of Athlone, the last surviving granddaughter of Queen Victoria. When Sir Hugh introduced us to her and told her that we lived on Herm Island she at once said "Oh, I remember Herm very well, our parents took us there when we were children. The Queen lent us her yacht. It *was* kind of her. We went up the south coast of England and across to Guernsey. A carriage was sent over to Herm and we went across and had a picnic on a long beach. I remember my brother and I gathered tiny little cowrie shells — they were *so* lovely."

Peter replied, "Well Ma'am if you were to go there now you would still be able to gather those same little shells."

She smiled delightedly, "Oh I'm so glad," and then added reflectively, "Prince Blucher von Waldstadt lived there in those days. He married Princess Radziwill."

This fascinating glimpse into history—touching as it did on our own island's story and from someone who had actually been living at the time was intriguing to say the least, and what was equally fascinating, not to say astonishing, was that this sprightly and totally delightful old lady remembered with such amazing clarity her Herm visit of what must have been at least 80 years ago.

I rarely walk along the Shell Beach today without thinking of that long ago picnic and picture the horse drawn carriage bowling across the Common; I wonder if the burnet roses were out, or was it when the golden bedstraw carpeted the ground?—and if she saw the wild bees busy amongst the purple thyme, as they are on any warm summer's day.

45
Today

Looking back across the years it seems now as if those first years were spent in a desperate search for sources of revenue. In fact our various enterprises add up to a formidable list; a pottery, flower growing, cottage industries such as weaving, shell work and pebble polishing; on the farm, milk production, new potato growing and pig rearing. And then there was our private island postal service and the Herm stamps. The stamps, in fact, were a very welcome source of revenue—albeit a very time consuming one for me—up until 1969 when Guernsey took over the postal services from the British Post Office, and Herm became a sub-post office—and Peter the sub-postmaster!

It seemed, in those early worrying days, to be the right and sensible thing to think up and do anything that would bring in money, but as time went on it came home to us that in most of these things we had no particular expertise or natural advantage. Now we are back to the two things that we do best; tourism and agriculture. Tourism in all its aspects for which the island is well suited, and dairy farming.

In addition to his interest in the farm, when constructional work is going on,—these days under Adrian's auspices—be it of repair or maintenance or some new project in the making, Peter likes to be on site from time to time to see the work going on and to feel concerned and involved with it, to see the possibilities of future development, and within the limits imposed by a back injury sustained a few years ago, to help physically in the actual work. Every now and again it is necessary for us to bring over a bulldozer to perform some of the heavier and larger of the tasks, chiefly those of site preparation for a proposed addition to a building, and at these times Pennie and I hold our breath in case Peter, and Adrian too, get carried away by their enthusiasm for 'pushing the frontiers further back' and some well loved nook and cranny or favourite tree stands in imminent danger and we find ourselves dashing out to take up, if not exactly belligerent, at least cautionary and defensive positions which is usually enough to ensure that moderation is maintained.

Most of all Peter takes pleasure from his involvement with people, both those who work for us and those who holiday on the island; he has no wish to dabble in their lives but he likes to know, we both do, that they know we are here and that we have a concern for their problems, both in their work and in their homes, and that we are available to them if they need us. It is a reciprocal thing for we also know that we can call on anyone of them for help should we need it. It is this feeling of interdependence that is important to us.

By the very nature of island life the community is a changing one. Children grow up and larger schools and horizons have to be sought, so in that respect it is not, perhaps, exactly as Peter visualised it when he wrote those wartime letters so long ago now; but there are some who have stayed with us on a more permanent basis. Dick, although he and Joan now live in Guernsey, comes across to us daily on the early morning Trident 'milk run'; and Joan too, to help on busy days. Along with Linda, another long time resident, he has managed the Gift Shop for us for many years, and it has flourished and expanded under their imaginative direction. But now, sadly, they too feel that it is time to move on and soon we shall be seeing new faces on the island. Stephanie has been with us too for 10 years, and John who looks after all the island gardens, and especially our own, although not the same 'John the Gardener' who was with us in the very early days, has nevertheless made Herm his home for the past 14 years.

Sadly Philip died three years ago. Although he and Nina had lived in Guernsey for some time they were always very closely associated with us and all that went on in Herm. Even now Peter finds himself thinking, 'I must remember to tell Phil that' or 'I'll ask Phil if he remembers how those pipes were laid' or 'where that cable runs', and most of all we miss his cheerful company. But perhaps he is still aware of all that we do. We feel that he is, and certainly like to think so.

The future, as the song says 'is not ours to see' and thinking about it in the past Peter and I often wondered which of the family would be most suitable to take on the management of the island, who, indeed, would be available when it became apparent that the time had come to share some of the load. Which of them would have the necessary skills, the necessary enthusiasm? The last ingredient was without doubt to be found in all of them. Simon was the first to take over the reins of management in 1974 and stayed with us in this capacity for over five years until in 1980 his children began to outgrow our small island school and he moved over to Guernsey. Who to follow him? This was at a time when Peter had been having a series of back problems and it was a relief when Pennie and Adrian suggested that they should come with Hannah their little daughter then age two. Adrian was a partner in a firm of Estate Agents and Managers in Guernsey so had the necessary skills and they were, it seemed prepared to make themselves available. We gladly accepted their suggestion. And now we often reflect how very fortunate we have been and still are, for Adrian and Pennie continue to intepret our schemes and dreams in a manner which we would never have thought possible. Their modus operandi is different—the end product the same. Looking further ahead still, we have no doubt that from among the ranks of our family, be he son or son-in-law, grandson or great grandson there will always be one who will carry on. Some one of us for whom the magical appeal of the island is a part of his very fabric, whose children's earliest memories, like his own and his parents' before him, will be of Herm, and who will grow up knowing the secret places where time has trod lightly and the passing centuries made little impress on the lovely contours of the land and the blowing flowers and grasses.